GERMAN
SUBMARINE
WARFARE

ABANDONMENT OF A SINKING VESSEL.

GERMAN SUBMARINE WARFARE

A STUDY OF ITS METHODS AND SPIRIT

INCLUDING

THE CRIME OF THE "LUSITANIA"
A RECORD OF OBSERVATIONS AND EVIDENCE

BY

WESLEY FROST
UNITED STATES CONSUL, FORMERLY STATIONED
AT QUEENSTOWN

WITH AN INTRODUCTION BY
FRANK LYON FOLK
COUNSELOR FOR THE DEPARTMENT OF STATE

ILLUSTRATED

UNIFORM

First published by D. Appleton & Company in 1918.
This edition first published by Uniform in 2018
an imprint of Unicorn Publishing Group

Unicorn Publishing Group
101 Wardour Street
London W1F 0UG
www.unicornpublishing.org

Copyright © Unicorn Publishing Group, 2018

A catalogue record for this book is available from the British Library

ISBN 978-1-910500-24-8

Printed and bound in Great Britain

Please note: *In producing in facsimile from original historical documents, any
imperfections may be reproduced and the quality may be lower than modern
typesetting or cartographic standards.*

DEDICATED TO

Robert P. Skinner
American Consul-General at London

My considerate superior officer and
helpful mentor during Queenstown days

PREFACE

UNDER THE RULES OF READY WRITING I SUPPOSE AN ANALYSIS OF German submarine methods should commence with some ghastly and gripping incident. But, with the reader's favor, I desire expressly to avoid that sort of introduction; both for a general reason and for a special reason.

In the first place such a study ought to be an appeal to mentality fully as much as to emotion. The emotional tug will be present whether designed or not. You will be unable, unless you are subnormal—or at least abnormal—to read the incidents us d as illustrations without a spontaneous revulsion of heart. The facts are passion-rousing facts. Therefore it becomes highly important, in dissecting them, to preserve the utmost possible detachment, and steadily to address the reader's intelligence. If a clean bill of indictment is to be brought in, the entire set of counts must be such as can go down into history as solid and veridical.

The second reason is quasi-personal. It happens to have fallen to my lot, in the line of duty, to talk publicly in many cities upon the *Unterseebooten*; and I have been a little oppressed by the inaccurate ideas which sometimes seem to have been left upon the popular mind. Confronted with the need of producing a correct and indelible impression by a few minutes' speech-making from a "standing start," any speaker is sometimes forced to resort to chiaroscuro or caricature in order to drive his points home into the minds of all classes of auditors. Then, too, the newspaper men have a fatal proclivity for giving a sensational twist to the most carefully guarded language; and statements have been placed in my mouth so weirdly distorted as to provoke good honest American skepticism from any average man. For example there have been generously inserted impassioned descriptions of how the submarine which sank the *Lusitania* emerged and hovered gloatingly about the scene, although I have never possessed or hinted at any reliable evidence that the submarine in the *Lusitania* case was observed to emerge at all. A zealous and impressionable young man in the Northwest caused his newspaper to state that the subject of my address was, "Buckets of Blood"; and it has occasionally seemed as though the entire Fourth Estate believes that only an appeal of the "Buckets of Blood" stripe can be effective in our democracy.

Thus I have developed a longing to have my say out quietly and *in extenso*, without the use of omissions or high lights. The discussion will be galvanic enough at best. Justice cannot be done in dealing with these subsea raparees without the production of data such as to shock and to inflame; and the greater the calmness that can be achieved the better.

Now when an earnest and candid man sits down to give his earnest and patient consideration to accusations so very grave as those which Humanity now levels against the German submarines, will not his first question be, "How has the truth of these alleged facts been established?" In other words is he not justified in a curiosity as to how the material which substantiates the charges has been gathered and authenticated? The answer must of course be affirmative. That is why it seems best to describe at the outset the manner in which the American consulates have worked in procuring evidence,—for any statements made regarding the Queenstown Consulate can be applied with minor variations to its sister offices abutting on the danger zone.

CONTENTS

LIST OF ILLUSTRATIONS

INTRODUCTION

THE EXTENT AND IMPORTANCE OF THE SUBMARINE ATROCITIES WHICH the American Consul at Queenstown was called upon to report to our Government during the period preceding our entry into the war are probably matters of general knowledge. As for the quality of the reports which were forthcoming in response to the exigency, the best evidence is the fact that a cablegram of commendation was sent to the Consul by the Secretary of State, an unusual expression of merit in the Consular Service.

Upon America's entry into the war the submarine depredations off Queenstown had no longer the significance which they had possessed when any one of them might constitute a *casus belli*; and in June, 1917, Consul Frost, whose health had suffered severely under the strain, was brought back to America upon furlough, and was assigned to duty in the Department of State. Almost before he could begin his new duties, however, the Committee on Public Information procured permission to requisition his services for publicity work; and, with the cooperation of the Chamber of Commerce of the United States, he was sent out to tell his story as the pioneer speaker in the Government's information campaign. The success of his tours, which extended throughout the west, southwest, and middle west, was immediate and striking. One of his first addresses became somewhat of an international classic on the subject; and has since done wide service, not only throughout the British Isles under the title "Devils of the Deep," but also in translations in French and Spanish countries under the respective titles "Les Assassins de la Mer" and "Le Guerra Submarina de Alemania."

It is rather fitting that the same American whose lot it was to be foremost in gathering evidence regarding submarine warfare should also be the first to furnish a comprehensive popular summary and interpretation of that evidence. Mr. Frost's work for Mr. Creel, moreover, had the effect of keeping the entire subject before his mind, and thus enabled him to thread his way judiciously through the pitfalls which must beset any officer of the Department of State who writes upon such a topic at just this juncture. His work, it is believed, will be found to constitute as good a general survey of the submarine campaign as is apt to be given to the public for a considerable time to come, and should rank among the great popular documents relating to the war.

Mr. Frost's work with reference to Germany's violations of well-recognized laws of marine warfare is indeed valuable, but it is in connection with Germany's deliberate crimes against the conscience of mankind that his testimony and conclusions have the greatest claim on our attention.

FRANK LYON POLK.

GERMAN SUBMARINE WARFARE

CHAPTER I

GATHERING THE EVIDENCE

THE *LUSITANIA* TRAGEDY PROVED TO BE ONLY THE BLACK HARBINGER to a whole harpy-flight of German crimes in South Irish waters. They came rather slowly at first, but their accelerating frequency gradually darkened our entire horizon. The Queenstown Consulate found itself faced with a sequence of duties and opportunities for service, it is safe to say, as strange as ever confronted a consular office.

The Atlantic Ocean between the Fastnet Rock Lighthouse and the Scilly Islands is, you will recall, the most crowded highway of commercial shipping on the globe. On a fine day I have stood upon the cliffs at Fortress Templebreedy and looked out to sea upon a perpetually shifting parade of steamships and sailing ships as far as the eye could reach. One glance at a trade-map will make clear how the vast capillary suck of commerce into Liverpool, Cardiff, Dublin and Glasgow pulls a majority of the vessels approaching the United Kingdom within something like a hundred miles of Queenstown. The converging sea-lanes from four continents furnish here a grand-scale demonstration of the world's waterborne commerce, and constitute the region an ideal theater for submarine operations. It was into this peaceful trade-sea that the German submersibles began their incursions, in the summer of

1915, to prey among the diligent merchantmen like sharks striking in among shoals of porpoises.

Queenstown inevitably took on forthwith a new importance and interest. Our beautiful little city, clinging against its steep green hillside by the most charming tidal harbor in the world, grew in a few months from a population of eight thousand to more than ten thousand people. It had always been famous for the picturesqueness of its streets, not only as a garrison town but as the British Naval headquarters for all Irish waters. In addition to the army and navy uniforms there were the Irish country-people, with their donkey carts and shawled women, as well as the omni-present priests and police and the merchant sailors from all lands. And now, as the German submarines pushed their forays nearer and nearer, and Queenstown became the clearing-house for survivors from their attacks, our streets gained a still further element of diversity in the groups of pathetic human salvage. We could hardly walk down Harbor Row without encountering men or women just saved from the ordeals of exposure and assault. Every street-child in Queenstown old enough to point and cry, "Soldier," or, "Sailor," learned to know also the word, "Survivor," and to apply it to these oddly clad figures.

In a single day, between midnight and midnight, in March of 1917, when the campaign was at its worst, we saw the survivors landed from no less than six different torpedoed ships! All in all, during my incumbency at Queenstown, that is up until June, 1917, two months after America entered the war, the Consulate made reports to the Secretary of State upon some eighty different submarine attacks in which American citizens or rights were imperiled or destroyed.

In between fifty and sixty of these cases we took detailed legal testimony. In many of the instances our witnesses were American passengers. Among the male passengers there were business men, journalists and authors, medical and professional men, and a good sprinkling of clerics; and among the female passengers there were wives of American officers or physicians, authoresses, actresses, nurses, and society women. In a greater number of instances the testimony came from American citizens serving in various capacities on foreign or American vessels for pay. Their competency as witnesses ranged all the way from that of negro or Filipino deckhands or coal-passers up to that of a high-salaried expert from one of America's greatest electrical firms. Quite a few British ships carried one or more American officers or petty officers — deck-officers, horse-foremen, boatswains, masters-at-arms, engineers, donkeymen, and galleymen. But whatever the rank, color, or social status of these American witnesses, they one and all came to the Consulate, at all hours of the day and night, straight from the sea, with the voices of their dead companions still ringing in their ears. They were examined while the occurrences were fresh and vivid in their minds.

The survivors were brought in to the Queenstown wharves on every variety of craft. Often they had been picked up by an Admiralty vessel, or had been transferred at sea to such a vessel from the original rescue ship. Thus a humble Admiralty trawler might be packed to the gunwales with the survivors from some large ship, while a destroyer, an armed sloop, or a mine-layer might bring in only a handful of sailors from a lost barque. Often, too, the rescue ship which came in to Queenstown would prove to be a swift passenger packet, a freight liner or tramp, a schooner or barkentine, or even a fishing boat. In two or three cases the lifeboats themselves came rowing right in, all the long way past the frowning fastnesses of Carlisle and Camden and the lovely promontory of Cork-a-Beg, and drew directly into the Queenstown cambers. Such boats were always welcomed by an admiring group of water-front habitués, old seamen who could appreciate their feat. If they had rowed back from midstream of the River Styx, as figuratively of course they had, they could hardly have evoked greater wonder and admiration.

In important cases the Consulate was usually notified by the Admiralty prior to the arrival of the 'ships carrying the survivors. We were thus able to be at the dock to greet the American victims and to have a preliminary talk with the surviving ship's officers. The *Laconia* survivors landed late at night, for example; and after a hasty conversation with Captain Ervine, I took two or three American survivors—one of whom was Floyd Gibbons of the *Chicago Tribune*—to the Consulate and fed them on sandwiches, chocolate and hot-flask tea while getting the facts from them right onto the typewriter in the form of cable reports. In the *Cymric* case we sat up all night, keeping in touch with Admiralty House, in order to get the Naval wireless reports onto the cable as rapidly as they came in. Then I took a morning train to Bantry, and met my friend Captain Beadnell and his men as they stepped onto the pier at four o'clock that afternoon. By five o'clock I had taken their formal statements, and by five-thirty had filed my cables. Our mailed dispatches in all these cases were of course the fruit of much subsequent investigation. In the *Cymric* case I did not finish checking up until noon of the second day; and in cases where more time was available, as it usually was, the inquiries were further protracted.

When we were not able to receive notice of arrival actually in advance we always got it immediately upon the advent of the survivors at the offices of the Queenstown shipping agents. The first act of the senior officer surviving in each group of victims on reaching Queenstown would be to take his men to the ship's agents; and the agents all very cordially helped the Consulate by letting us know if there were any Americans affected—saved or lost—and by sending the American survivors promptly to the Consulate. We tried not to let the responsibility for such notifications fall upon their busy shoulders, and took the initiative daily in keeping in touch with them. We also made frequent inquiries upon the Royal Irish Constabulary and, if occasion presented, upon the Admiralty. I think hardly an American was landed at Queenstown from a torpedoed ship without finding himself at the Consulate within an hour's time.

The personal needs of these victims were almost invariably attended to efficiently by the ships' agents, at the expense of the ships' owners. Food, lodging, medical attendance and new clothing were provided with the utmost good will and energy. Transportation to England was usually furnished by the Shipwrecked Mariners Society; and scores, if not hundreds, of American seamen profited by this broadminded practice. The regulations by which Queenstown is partially closed to shipping, and is wholly closed to the embarkation or debarkation of non-British persons, made it almost indispensable for the survivors to proceed to some English port to take a new ship; but this worked no financial hardship either upon passengers or seamen.

The condition of the survivors on arrival at Queenstown was often pitiable; but, strange to say, in only rather few cases was it really grave. Victims who had been drowned or killed by shellfire were commonly buried at sea; and such wounded persons as remained alive until they reached Queenstown had usually received only minor injuries. The hospital cases, therefore, were apt to have arisen from flesh-wounds due to bombardment or from accidents or explosions during the attack. Superficial contusions and broken bones were not infrequent. The cases of exhaustion from exposure yielded to warmth, food, and rest.

The survivors from passenger vessels were as a rule more wretched than those from freight vessels. The grief-stricken members of decimated families added an element of distress; and owing to the presence of women and children there were more stretcher cases and cases of dangerous collapse. And from passenger ships the corpses were often brought in. It would be almost a sacrilege for me to describe these poor clayey integuments of humanity for the purpose of working upon your feelings. We had often occasion to be honestly thankful for that queer, puzzled peacefulness which stamps the faces of the drowned.

The naval and military surgeons were ably assisted and supplemented by local medical men and by Red Cross—V. A. D.— units. In fact there was customarily a redundancy of medical and surgical skill at hand.

These facts, especially as to the efforts of the ships' agents, left the Consulate comparatively little to do in the way of tangible humanitarian duties, at least after the first big cases which caught us all off our guard. We loaned a good deal of money, usually on behalf of the Embassy funds; and occasionally interceded with various authorities for some trivial adjustment, always cheerfully accorded. We also sent messages to survivors' friends in the United States, and tried in personal ways to cheer and relieve our afflicted fellow-countrymen. But the pictures which have sometimes been painted in the American press of our Consulate's staff in the role of ministering angels have really been much overdrawn.

In this connection I may mention that the fortitude and determined cheerfulness exhibited by the survivors were perpetual sources for pleasure and pride. In cases where there were no fatalities the predominant note was one of hearty courage and good fellowship. The sailor-boys would score jokes off one another's petty misfortunes with all the lightheartedness which is said to mark the trench wit of the Doughboys and Tommies. Especially was this true of the professional seamen. Commend me to a sailor for a certain frank upstanding manliness which landsmen — or certainly many city men — seem to miss. The fact that the English are a seafaring people must surely account in no small measure for their retention of national stamina. The seas are England's lungs, which renew and oxygenate her racial character.

Regarded as witnesses the American passengers showed every shade of responsibility and irresponsibility. I take the liberty of dwelling upon this feature in order that the reader may be assured that proper discounting was made as to the reliability of each piece of testimony. The lady passengers, we found, made either very good or very poor witnesses. Whenever the feminine quality of patience, which causes women to be such good mathematicians and linguists, could be brought into play we secured very much accurate detail — sometimes too much detail and too little discrimination as to vital features. Perhaps this last observation applies equally to both sexes, for quite a few of the masculine as well as the feminine passengers took delight in recounting minutely their own personal adventures and experiences during the disasters. Such statements were excellent exemplifications of what is known by psychologists as the phenomenon of total recall. Amid the welter of irrelevant facts in these narratives there would often appear bits of highly germane evidence; and the authenticity of such portions was all the better for the mass of meticulous *trivia* in which they were embedded.

The newspaper men, some of whom were present at almost every passenger catastrophe, made the very best witnesses we had. They are trained at making and taking mental note of their observations. The next class in responsibility was that of the business men; presumably because they are accustomed to dealing in the practical and the concrete. On the whole we were rather disappointed in the statements elicited from the professional men. Their characters, if not their faculties, seemed to be a trifle too highly sensitized and to lack the matter-of-factness which makes for the soundest legal demonstration.

In turning to the American witnesses from freight vessels this last distinction is also useful, . at least by analogy. Those-of the seamen, horse-tenders, and firemen who had some smattering of education or sophistication were eager and responsive; but their observations did not appear to be quite so trustworthy as those of the men who had always earned their livelihoods by stern physical labor. Especially did we learn to distrust the city boys, who seemed either to be runaway readers of Nick Carter fiction or else, in a few cases, flashy slum-rats with not quite enough wits to maintain themselves in the underworld at home.

But I must hasten to emphasize that in every aggregation of survivors we were able to find adequate sources of the most dependable kind of testimony. We soon learned to identify the most valuable members of each group, and seldom failed to get satisfactory details. We checked up the survivors' stories individually against one another in many cases, and sometimes made corrections in this way. The American witnesses were inclined to be more shocked and repelled by the conduct of the submarines than were the Europeans; and this formed a minor reason why we took the utmost pains in nearly every case to get the deposition of the British or Scandinavian ships' officers.

The primary reason for taking officers' affidavits lay in the superior knowledge and skill which officers possess as to all technical sea matters; and their testimony also had great value merely as corroborating the American testimony. We came to feel quite a little confidence in our devices for testing and appraising the various evidence; and I can therefore allow myself to express the opinion that the Norwegian and English licensed mariners are the most inveterate tellers of sober-daylight truth that can anywhere be encountered. Time and again I have heard them testify in the most stolid and matter-of-fact manner to facts which might easily have been omitted or modified to damage the German side of the case or strengthen the Allied side. The innate taciturnity of the northern races seems to have as its complement a self-possessed and unimaginative truthfulness in whatever statements these men do permit themselves to emit.

Although they are inclined to be both positive and pertinacious they are careful and reasonable. I remember a master who insisted that the torpedo had absolutely transpierced the hull of his ship and had been seen by him to emerge on the far side while exploding. Of course a torpedo, with its comparatively light weight and slow speed, can never acquire the momentum to penetrate very far into a ship before it explodes; and this fact we tried tactfully to bring out. It was curious to see the manner in which the captain consented to take our point of view under advisement, as it were; and the mixture of frankness and reluctance with which he eventually admitted that his observation must have been mistaken.

How heedfully the Consulate tried to work in discarding questionable testimony may be illustrated by the way the advent of the supersubmarines was handled. Supersubmarine stories began to rear their heads among the narratives of the less reliable seamen and stokers as early as July, 1916; and we took care to go into each one and dispose of it by the evidence from professional American seamen and from the ships' officers. This had occurred, at infrequent intervals, for so many months that we developed a settled idea that the diving-cruiser was to remain a myth. We came to classify it mentally with the detonation of distant explosives by wireless "purple rays," if not actually with the Cape Cod sea-serpent. I was accordingly brought up all standing one day in the spring of

1917 when a British master of very solid type testified that the submarine which had sunk his ship had been over three hundred feet in length. I turned to the chief engineer, and said, half-jokingly, "You are a Scotchman and a natural skeptic, besides being a man who deals in mechanical precision. You won't support any such Jules Verne tale?" But he answered simply, "It's God's truth, Mr. Frost. She *was* three hundred feet long." Ten days later came the startling jump in the weekly figure of sinkings to forty-two ships of over sixteen hundred tons. The blue-water submarines had really arrived.

In the taking of so much testimony there were bound to be occasional little diverting incidents, such as go to swell the fund of court-room anecdotal humor. It is no disparagement of the negro race to say that the negro seamen often seemed anxious principally to give whatever answers they thought might please us best. There was a tendency on the part of British West India black boys, frequently found among these crews along with American negroes, to claim American origin, apparently for the purpose of gaining the earnest attention of an official for their stories, or for the purpose of having the solemn thrill of being placed upon oath. Out of several instances of this kind I recall especially one husky and dusky chap, with rolling bloodshot eyes, who burst into the office in a fine state of induced exhilaration. He boomed out, in a superb African bass voice, "Ah wants mah Consul," and proceeded to try to interest us in his tale of submarine disaster. Two or three well-placed questions by Mr. Thompson, the Vice-Consul, were enough to show that he was a Bahama boy.

During the last months of my incumbency at Queenstown we began to get "repeats," or men whom we had interviewed in previous cases. We saw a dozen different men who had "been torpedoed" as many as three times; and heard of men who had figured in four or even five submarine incidents. One stoker witness came to the Consulate in excellent clothing, so that I remarked casually, "I see you have been to the stores already for your new outfit." "Not at all, Sir," he answered; "this was my third time at being torpedoed; and so when she sighted the submarine I went below and put on all my good clothes, knowing we should save only what we stood up in."

In the case of the *Canadian* last spring, we went down to the wharf to meet the survivors in a drizzle and fog. I touched on the arm, with some introductory query, the first man I could locate in the throng with an officer's uniform. He turned around, and I shall never forget the pained and wounded expression with which he replied, "Why, don't you know me, Mr. Frost? I'm Dr. Patrick Burns, whose affidavit you took in the *Iberian* case. I've been taking notes for you all through this affair; and was looking forward to your knowing me." A second look beneath the stubble beard and grime revealed the genial face of this energetic American ship's surgeon whom I had sworn in relation to the *Iberian* case nearly two years previously. And he had actually been taking notes for me *from* the moment the attack had commenced, as imperturbably as if he had been at a clinic in a New England hospital.

Not all the persons rescued after submarine attacks off Ireland came to Queenstown. Quite frequently crews or passengers would be landed at Castletown Berehaven, famed for its copper mines, at Bantry, which is almost as truly "the home of beauty" as Killarney, at Schull, a wild fisher village, or at Cahirciveen, where the Atlantic Cable emerges. In these cases the survivors usually went through to England without making the rail detour to Queenstown, and we were forced to hasten up to Cork or Mallow to take their statements while they were making train connections at those junction-points. Sometimes only thirty or forty minutes were available. In three or four cases it was only possible to collect provisional material while jolting rapidly in an Irish jaunting-car from one railway station at Cork to another. Eight or ten times we went to the Sailors' Home at Cork and interviewed our men in a fine deep-sea atmosphere of boiled cabbage and pig's head. Then it would be necessary to dash off to a nearby hotel and talk with the officers while the latter were attacking their first respectable meal on shore just before their train was to leave.

Needless to say the affidavits procured in this hustled fashion were mailed to their makers for revision and confirmation, or were confirmed by supplementary affidavits taken by the consular offices at Liverpool, London, or Cardiff. But there were surprisingly few corrections. A rapid-fire of carefully prepared questions launched at a group of seamen engaged in tucking away honest provender seems to dislodge the plain truth almost automatically, without any chance for distortion born of irritation or imagination. The men would correct one another noisily, and thresh out a point among themselves in thirty seconds, so as to give me a consensus which stood the test of any amount of subsequent checking up either by myself or by my eminent colleague, Consul Horace Lee Washington of Liverpool. In fact I think that the staccato, impromptu character of these interviews constituted a real guaranty of their *bona fides*.

The procedure followed by the Queenstown Consulate in conducting investigations as to submarine outrages is not unlike that in a dozen other consulates. In addition to the fine affidavits prepared by Consul Washington and Vice Consul Watson at Liverpool — which will be permanent memorials as to the induction of America into the war-great service has been given by the consular offices at London, Algiers, Havre, Malta and Cardiff, and to a somewhat less degree by those at Bristol, Glasgow, La Rochelle, Marseilles and Belfast.

The submarine campaign, as depicted by the affidavits taken by the Consular Service, constitutes America's principal overt grievance against Germany; and of course it is also one of the most significant features of the general German spirit against which the entire civilized world is warring. The degree of credence which is yielded to the consular evidence is thus an important matter. As to the Queenstown office I shall always like to believe that, in addition to the unusually large number of important cases handled by us, there was one especial case—an incredibly abominable submarine crime—which formed the actual precipitating cause of President Wilson's decision to declare war. But this is only conjecture.

The various consuls have undoubtedly possessed somewhat varying points of view of a nature to affect their work of evidence-gathering. In my own case, as in that of many of my colleagues, it happened that, being a man of legal training, I took a professional pride in conducting these inquiries with juridical impartiality. Most consuls of the newer school, too, have doubtless like myself been imbued with the peace-idealism of the past fifteen years in America; and have doubtless learned a rather special love for the country which we serve. Thus our entire original bias, if it must be admitted that any bias existed, was toward minimizing the German misdeeds, and toward explaining them away, in order to avert war from America.

In my own case there was even a further influence. It chances that a year of my boyhood was spent in the Fatherland, and left me with a deep-rooted liking and admiration for all things German. I attended the *Volkschulen*, snapped beans with the other boys at recess-times, and partook in due course both in the school walking-tours and in the rattan-discipline. I have the pleasantest possible memories of the little cornucopias of cherries, the good-humored soldiers who mounted guard at the door of the Colonel who lodged below us, and the fascinating play-days around the old tannery where Prince von Bismarck roomed in his student days. To this day if I were awakened from a profound sleep, to hear the word "German" I believe my mechanical cortical reaction would be one of warm cordiality.

It will be evident that I was not at the outset of the war precisely a prejudiced medium for discovering German atrocities where none existed. It was only the ceaseless avalanche of facts pouring in upon me week after week and month after month which gradually convinced me that something has come over the German, people in Germany. "Facts are stubborn things"; and I have found myself, as a conscientious commissioned officer, constrained to bear faithful testimony that the German submarine campaign has been carried on with a depravity and degradation which we could not have foreseen and would not have believed of the German people.

And now we may allow ourselves to turn to a general exposition of the methods and spirit of the campaign as shown by the consular affidavits. It is worth noting that the most critical and crucial period of he campaign was comprised by the early months of 1917. The restraints of humanity and of the law of nations were increasingly discarded by the submarines during the summer and autumn of 1916; and at the beginning of February, 1917, when the unrestricted warfare was announced, the announcement was merely a shameless avowal of a policy already in vigor. The submarine attacks during the winter and early spring of 1917 attained a quality which America could no longer overlook. It is these attacks, accordingly, which will receive the closest scrutiny from historians of the Great War.

The statements, illustrative incidents and expressions of opinion given below are based in the main upon Queenstown investigations, and special attention has been bestowed upon the critical period just indicated. The Queenstown Consulate had no connection with several important cases, such as the *Falaba, Sussex,* and *Persia;* of course the large amount of evidence which we did accumulate—and it was large not only positively but relatively—was not sufficient on some points to permit conclusive deductions. Therefore I have not hesitated to refer occasionally to corroborative cases handled by other consulates, and even to facts which came to our knowledge at Queenstown informally.

For convenience in treatment, the German manner, or practical tactics, of conducting the U-boat campaign may be considered under five general groups or divisions, although something will then remain to be said regarding the spirit of the campaign. The five groups are as follows:

(1) The manner of attack upon unarmed ships, usually sailing-ships or the poorer class of steamships. In cases involving such vessels the submarines have been able to emerge and maneuver freely on the surface of the sea, with very scant misgivings as to danger. Thus the submarine nature has had rather free scope to display itself.

(2) The manner of attack upon freight ships of fair size, which might be presumed to be armed. In cases of this class the submarines have done their work while submerged, and have used torpedoes instead of shellfire or bombs. This class of cases is of course by far the heaviest and most important at the present time (March, 1918).

(3) The fact as well as manner of attack upon ships which might be presumed to carry passengers. The large size of passenger liners, and the ethical and legal aspects of cases involving them, obviously place such cases in a class by themselves.

(4) The manner in which the submarines treat survivors while still on the scene of the attacks, either in the life-boats or in

the water. The personal demeanor of the U-boat officers and men toward their victims is fairly uniform, irrespective of whether the vessel concerned belongs to the first, second, or third of the above classes.

(5) The fact as well as the manner of leaving survivors to the mercy of the elements far away from land. This feature, also, is common to the attacks upon all three classes of ships, and may therefore be separated off and dealt with distinctly.

CHAPTER II

DEFENSELESS SHIPS

THE PRESENCE OF SAILING-SHIPS, AND OF UNARMED SHIPS GENERALLY, in the danger zone is now a thing of the past; but such ships were plentiful in the zone up until midsummer of 1916, and were there in some numbers even as late as the summer of 1917. The German submarines in attacking these vessels enjoyed ample facilities for working unhampered, without the fear of guns or speed on the part of their victims to cramp their natural impulses or methods.

And in the early days of the war, to be quite fair, it was the ordinary custom of the submersibles to warn a sailing-ship or small steamer by two or three wide shots. When the vessel heaved to — which these crafts have always done with the utmost alacrity — the submarine would hail or signal an order to take to the lifeboats. It would then stand passively and contentedly by, and give the crew whatever amount of time they needed to commence as favorably as possible their dire struggle to reach the land. A typical case was that of the Cardiff barque *Cardonia*, a coal carrier. She sighted a submarine twenty-four miles off a famous Irish landmark, in April, 1916, in moderate weather. The U-boat fired two shots, palpably designed merely as a warning to heave to. The *Cardonia* of course complied, and the Germans then approached and informed the master that he might take thirty minutes to abandon his ship, or more if he could show a reason. Later, when the ship had been abandoned, the submarine came up to the lifeboats in friendly fashion and gave them correct and helpful advice about making for the land.

While this case was typical of the period in which it occurred, there did transpire brutal cases even then. When the least undue dilatoriness was imputed to the master of an attacked ship in taking to the boats the submarine made no bones about firing repeatedly, sometimes through the rigging. Indeed, when *any* broad statement is made as to just which kind of practices were prevalent at the various stages of the campaign, it must be understood that numerous exceptions can always be cited against such a generalization.

But in a majority of the cases of attacks upon defenseless ships up until the autumn of 1916 there was no ill conduct on the part of the submarines. The latter were usually in rather good spirits at finding such easy victims, and often permitted themselves a few half-ironical amenities with the men whom they were about to desert on the sea. There occur to me the cases of the *Chancellor, Hesione* and *Anglo-Columbian* as showing what the Germans could do, when they wished, in the way of decency. Such cases indicate the manner in which the campaign would have been permanently carried on if it had been in the hands of most civilized peoples.

For as the campaign progressed, and notably during the late summer and the autumn of 1916, the submarines' manner of dealing with these helpless little steamers or sailers became increasingly harsh and sharp. Instead of firing two or three warning shots they would fire six or eight, aimed apparently to hit the ship. Instead of allowing such time as seemed desirable for taking to the boats they began to set very narrow time limits—fifteen, ten, or even five minutes—and to enforce these limits with Draconian rigor. For example the steamship *Tottenham*, hailing from Baltimore, Maryland, was attacked on August 3, 1916; and the ten-minute time limit imposed upon her had not quite expired when the submarine began shelling her continuously.

By the end of 1916 and the early part of 1917 the U-boat men were plunging deeper and deeper into inhumanity. Their so-called warnings had degenerated in the main into unremitting and vicious bombardments without pause or pity. They had ceased to hail, assist, or instruct their victims at all; at least until the crews had taken to the boats in frantic haste under a steady fusillade, and had come well clear of the vessels.

A full-rounded example of this natural ultimate of the policy which had been evolving is the case of the *Madura*. The *Madura* was a little Russian barque carrying creosoted pine timber from Pensacola, Florida; and was attacked by a submarine just before noon one day in the spring of 1917. The weather was not really severe, although there was a stiff spring breeze and the waves were choppy. The submersible appeared less than a half-mile astern, and promptly began a merciless shellfire. The master of the *Madura* signaled submission instantly, even going so far as to cut down his mainsail upon the submarine's first shot. The submarine utterly ignored this pitiable self-abasement. It came up shooting, and continued to fire incessantly into the *Madura*.

Thirty minutes later when the *Madura's* lifeboat was rescued by a friendly craft it was a perfect shambles. The master, a huge black-bearded Finn, sat safely in the stern-sheets with his wife beside him; but at their feet two dead sailors lay weltering in blood, and a third was just coughing out his life. Four other occupants of the boat were gory with lacerations from shrapnel. These inoffensive working men had been slaughtered and torn after they had surrendered, and while they were trying desperately to comply with any command the Prussians might have been graciously pleased to manifest.

I can cite you instance after instance like this, in which a frail and unarmed craft has made submission and pleaded for quarter, like a little dog that rolls over on its back and begs, and then has been pounded and raked with shellfire, sometimes with the most sickening casualties. Here are a few: The *Tungstan, Gaspian, Dalbeattie, Galgorm Castle, Lynton, Valkyrie, Hainault, Storstad, Cairnhill, Rowanmore, Iberian, Vanduara, Margareta, Alice, Margam Abbey, Wallace, Lucy Anderson, 'Arethusa* and *Carnmoney.* In many of these cases there were casualties, and in some of them fatalities, from the pitiless shellfire.

This list could be greatly amplified, but should suffice to establish the fact of wanton bombardments against unarmed ships. Like any creature which depends upon stealth for security, and is thus a natural coward, the submarine exhibits the meanest type of cruelty the moment stealth becomes unnecessary. I usually think of the German U-boats as selachians—*genus squalus,* Linn.—but the shark, after all, is no petty—minded coward; and I dare say Winston Churchill's phrase "water-rats" is better in the present connection.

The changing character of the German use of gunfire became apparent only gradually, and for several months we were puzzled about its purpose. We could not bring ourselves to realize that it was malignantly intended. One or two shots across a ship's bow are merely due notice, and three or four are legitimate warning. Beyond that number the firing may assume successively the aspect of admonishment, threat, and finally bombardment. We were loath to believe that the last-named stage had been reached.

In the first place bombardment seemed perfectly pointless, since we knew that the vessels were habitually surrendering precipitately upon the submarines' initial shots. Certainly the firing could not be designed either to overcome or to punish resistance.

In the second place if they were really trying to sink the ships or kill the occupants the firing seemed surprisingly ineffective for the Teuton arch-exponents of efficiency. Out of twenty or thirty shots fired at a vessel only four or five hits would be scored, and some of these would merely scamp the sticks or superstructures. In case after case, too, there would be no fatalities, and even no casualties. It seemed incredible that the proceeding was murderously intended when it actually issued in so little murder.

Like most civilians I had an undue faith in the unerring precision and deadly efficacy of what has been advertised as modern scientific warfare; and was therefore misled by the dearth of results from the submarine shellfire attacks. It was only after the evidence began to be unmistakably copious that I remembered that only one bullet out of many hundred in land warfare finds its target, and recalled Clausewitz' dictum that every act of war is at best but "action in a resisting medium."

For it gradually became quite clear that the Germans were really doing their best, or worst, in the way of shellfire against ships. Their firing simply was ineffective. In the case of the *Swanmore* they fired over two hundred shots, and were finally compelled to use a torpedo. Four Americans were killed, it may be parenthetically said. In the case of the *Iriston* the submarine fired fourteen shots from less than one hundred yards' distance, and then resorted to a torpedo. At the *Seatonia* twelve shots were fired from a distance of something over a mile, and not one of them scathed the ship. These cases are cited at random, and more could be picked up almost endlessly. Of course instances did occur in which shellfire did succeed in sinking ships; but the only one which comes to mind was that of an abandoned ship into which the submarine fired at pointblank range whenever the rolling of the seas exposed surfaces far below the waterline. Therefore, in my opinion, it may be stated definitely that shellfire from the guns which were carried by German submarines prior to the year 1917 could not sink even a sailing ship except at close range. Firing from any distance over one-half mile, the submarines' guns missed their marks entirely as a usual thing; and when they did hit they hit virtually at haphazard. An excellent illustration of poor submarine gunnery in American waters is the attack on the tug *Perth Amboy* and her barges, off Cape Cod, on July 21, 1918. If newspaper accounts are correct the submarine took an hour to sink the first one of its five targets, and was forced to approach to one hundred yards' distance, although the sea was calm.

Not that the Germans counted upon this deficiency to soften the severity of their attacks. The great purpose of these wanton bombardments, as you will now be in a position to understand, was the terrorizing of the crews of the ships attacked. The idea was to induce among the merchant seamen of all nations a strong horror of entering the zone infested by the submarines. And in order to compass this purpose it was desirable that as many deaths and injuries as possible might result from the shelling. These casualties were not desired so much for their own sake as because they might prove a means to the more important end of excluding all but the most reckless freight ships from the waters around th British Isles. But they were explicitly desired, nevertheless, and the slaughter wrought by the bombardments must bear the odium of being willful. An added incentive was the effect of shellfire in frequently rendering uninhabitable vessels which no amount of shelling would have been able to sink. By sacrificing the lives of a few more victims the submarines were thus able to save the cost of using torpedoes, for they could by bombardment drive the occupants out of a ship and send a party to sink her by bombs.

And as the cases multiplied there did eventually appear a sufficient quantity of maiming and murder by gunfire to give rationality to the "frightfulness" motive for these superficially purposeless bombardments. However conscious the submarines might be of the low efficiency of their shooting it never became necessary for them to give up hope, and they never did give up hope, of producing at least an appreciable amount of damage and death, and hence of terror. We encountered enough fatalities to be sure that they might reasonably believe the frightfulness policy to have a measurable effectiveness.

To give the final verification to this conclusion we presently commenced to get quite a few cases in which the shelling ceased as soon as the lifeboats were clear of the ships. This showed that when once the occupants had left a vessel the submarines no longer cared to pour shrapnel into it! Conceivably someone might say that if the firing were intended to kill and terrorize seamen it ought to have been extended to the lifeboats when they were clear of the ship. But to m mind the fact that the submarines did not-ordinarily-have quite the will to do this is merely evidence that after all the Germans were still human beings with some human instincts. I therefore regard the cases in which the submarines lost interest in firing at a ship as soon as her crew had gotten away from her—Cases like the *Lynton*, *Strathtay*, *Galgorm Castle*, and *Eagle Point*—as legitimate indications that the underlying purpose of the fusillades against unarmed ships was terrorism by means of death and danger.

I do not mean to assert that there were no cases in which the firing was due merely to nervousness or flusteredness; or that there were no cases in which the commanders fired, as it were, out of excess of precaution, with a general idea expressed by the vernacular phrase of "hurry-up regardless." But as a broad policy the development of systematic cannonades against helpless ships was inspired by a belief in *Schrecklichkeit* pure and simple.

A clean-cut case of frightfulness shellfire was that of the Lane&McAndrew steamship *Saxonian*, a cotton ship of twenty-eight hundred tons register, laden at Port Arthur, Texas. She was unarmed, and she carried no wireless apparatus. At a quarter past five o'clock one evening in February, 1916, when still two hundred and eighty miles from southwest Ireland, the *Saxonian* was fired upon by a submarine from about three-fourths of a mile off her port bow. The weather was moderately rough, and night was closing down. The *Saxonian* stopped her engines instantly, and heaved to; and the crew began to take to the boats in frantic haste. The shelling continued relentlessly, although the submarine could not possibly have failed to see that the vessel was being abandoned. At that stage in the campaign there was hardly any reason why the submarine should suspect any ship of carrying a gun, and the unarmed condition of the *Saxonian* was of course apparent as soon as she failed to reply to the submarine's shots.

And here took place an episode worth recounting. A Pennsylvania boy named James Weygand, a clean-cut, brown-eyed young fellow twenty years of age, was serving on the *Saxonian* as a fireman. During the bombardment he arrived at the top of the ladder leading down to the boats just ahead of the ship's boatswain, a man of middle age. Under the circumstances Weygand might have hurried down ahead of the boatswain without exciting the faintest comment; but although the shells were whining about them he stepped gallantly and promptly aside and let the elder man precede him toward safety. And by a whimsey of fate while both men were on the ladder against the ship's side a German shell burst behind them and killed the boatswain instantly, while Weygand escaped with two painful flesh wounds.

As a classic instance of virtue proving to carry its own reward this incident might grace the pages of Oliver Optic; but, entirely aside from that aspect, I recall no case in which Mrs. Frost and I took more pleasure in hospital visits. Our hero compatriot from Hatboro is a German-American, but as in the case of the vast majority of German-Americans we were proud to have him as a fellow-countryman;

CHAPTER III

SHIPS WHICH ATTEMPT TO ESCAPE

AN ARGUMENT SOMETIMES PUT FORWARD ABOUT THESE VILLAINOUS shellfire attacks upon defenseless ships is that they may be the result of belief by the submarines that the ships are in reality disguised fighting vessels or decoys. Our periodicals have mentioned from time to time the use by the Allies of so-called Q-boats or "mystery-ships" which conceal deadly armament under an apparently innocent exterior. If a submarine is apprehensive that it has to deal with such a craft its ethical rights with regard to shellfire are beyond dispute excellent.

This argument, by the way, too, is typical of quite a number which one hears emitted occasionally in smoking compartments, club rooms, or hotel lobbies. They are usually delivered either in confidential whispers or else, for contrast, by some loud talker who makes the innuendo that our execration of submarine methods is merely for popular consumption and is unworthy the credulity of four-footed adult males. Such arguments deserve to be dragged out for public scrutiny whenever they can be found.

In the present instance the answer is almost too obvious to call for statement. If a U-boat really had any idea that it had encountered a Q-boat it would not think of attempting to come to the surface and attack by shellfire; it would remain submerged and use torpedoes. In case the supposed merchant ship were actually thought to be a wolf in sheep's clothing the submarine would never expose itself by undertaking a bombardment, but would resort to its peculiar immunities in a subsea attack. Thus it is clear that while the fear of mystery-ships may in rare instances account for the use of torpedoes without warning it has no relevance whatever as an excuse for cruel fusillades against surrendered ships.

Another and weightier argument, propounded by the German chancellery itself, is that a vessel which seeks to escape from a submarine places herself outside the protection of international law. It has been a rule of the laws of war that an innocent merchant ship is bound to submit to visit and search by a belligerent vessel of war, and must not seek to evade it. A non-combatant vessel which is so unwilling to undergo examination that it resorts to flight may be attacked by a war vessel to compel submission, and may even be destroyed. Accordingly the Germans have piously pleaded injured innocence or traduced rectitude whenever taken to task for shelling a ship which has tried to escape.

But this rule of the *jus gentium* has two sides to it. In return for the quiet obedience of a merchant ship its adversary is bound not to sink the ship unless it carries contraband, and in any event to respect the lives of the civilian seamen and passengers. Even if a raider or blockader can establish, by careful search and by documents, his right to seize—or if unavoidable to sink—the victim-ship, he is still bound under the familiar formula of the texts "to place her occupants in safety, and see that they are landed at a convenient port."

© Copyright by Committee on Public Information

AN AMERICAN DESTROYER RESCUING THE CREW
OF A TORPEDOED TRANSPORT.

And it is not from this civilized visit and search that ships' crews try to escape in the present war. They try to escape from being hustled with violence into fragile open boats and left to be the sport of ocean tempests. In some cases the German brand of visit and search carries savageries even worse than this refined cruelty, as will appear presently. In other words the Germans have never for a single day carried out their side of the international code. They have from the first claimed the right of setting harmless non-combatants adrift in small boats at any distance from land. And yet with all the ignoble cunning of Shylock they have claimed their pound of flesh in dealing with America about attempted flight by submarine victims. As though the pitiable attempts of unarmed ships to make a run for safety gave to the iron *squalidae* a license to slay and destroy to the top of their bent!

I saw the dismembered fragments of the master of the *Anglo-Californian*, Captain Archibald Panlow, carried ashore in a burlap gunny-bag early on a dismal February morning in 1916, with the mangled bodies of eight of his men. Gouts of their flesh and long splashes of their blood plastered the bridge- deck of their ship. The crime for which they died was that they preferred a chance at escape to a certainty of being hounded into little boats in wild weather and left alone on the face of the deep.

There was the *Iberian*, too, whose navigators yielded for a few moments to the Nature-implanted impulse toward self-preservation. In the course of the "disciplinary" firing which the submarine administered to check this improper effort to fly, six of the *Iberian's* men were killed and eight were wounded. One of the dead men was a Yankee horse-foreman, — a Bostonian named Mark Wylie.

The shellfire which was poured into the *Rowanmore* and the *Dalbeattie* may have been gratuitous, of course, but was probably provoked by the pathetic attempts of these ships to get away. It is worth mentioning that in each of these cases there were several witnesses who believed that the firing was aimed at the lifeboats as well as the ship.

In other cases there has been no question at all but that the Germans have fired upon lifeboats because vessels have sought to escape. Supposedly they are vindicating the rules of international law and defending the right of visit and search! In the case of the *Eavestone* the submarine raked the lifeboats in a spiteful temper because the old collier had tried to stoke up and knock an extra knot or two out of her decrepit engines.

The *Eavestone*, a craft of only one thousand and sixty-three tons, outward bound from Barry Docks, Cornwall, to the Mediterranean, was attacked at noon in February, 1917, when ninety-five miles off the Fastnet. Her injudicious valor in trying to give the submarine a run seemed to irritate the superman in charge of the latter quite beyond his super self-control. He brought his craft rushing up to the poor little *Eavestone*, firing at every jump. The *Eavestone'*s men tumbled into their two gigs and pulled pluckily away from the ship. As soon as they came clear of the stern the submarine turned her gun upon them, finding their range by trial shots, and then shot down the master, the steward, the donkey-man, and two seamen. One of the seamen was a Baltimore negro named Richard Wallace. Thus did Germany punish the lawless wretches who had outraged the rules of marine warfare by trying to escape from the Prussian rendering of the practice of visit and search. Incidentally it may be guessed that a little *furor Teutonicus* possibly entered into the "incident." I was told that the sight of that reeking lifeboat would have turned a man's stomach.

Now a further serious *quaere* arises. Conceding that the right of flight from submarine attack is an elemental and indubitable one, does the merchant ship have any further rights in its encounters with these self-appointed custodians of international good usage? If it be wrong and unlawful for the submarines to set non-combatants afloat on the treacherous ocean wastes, as I hope to show in discussing our fifth general division, must it not be right and lawful for the intended victims to save themselves not merely by flight but by active resistance? For unmolested desertion to the elements is the very best that these victims can anticipate—a bare chance for life. And in many cases—*vide* section 4—they face actions which would make De Quincy yearn to rewrite his famous essay on Murder as a Fine Art. In fighting against the U-boats they are therefore unquestionably fighting for their lives; and self defense has spelled exculpation since mankind framed codes of justice and graved them onto stone before the earliest dawn of human history.

But Admiral Von Tirpitz and his satellites have had a different view. To their minds the fact that a freight ship has been guilty of fiendishly mounting a little gun for self-defense, and wickedly trying to use it when the U-boat undertakes its benign work of shelling the crew into lifeboats for abandonment, places that ship wholly outside the pale of common human considerations. If a vessel carries a gun the submarines feel freed from any vestigial notion that her occupants are fellow-men!

Take the case of the *East Wales*. This steamship of less than three thousand tons register was attacked by shellfire from two German submarines at six o'clock in the morning in moderate autumn weather in October, 1917. She mounted a defensive gun aft; and proceeded to make a gallant Fabian fight, handling her weapon so smartly that her pursuers kept their distance. In fact one of them presently,

"Bethought herself and went,

Having that within her womb which had left her ill content."

At least so we hope. But the other U-boat eventually proved to be too much for the merchant fighters. Under a steady grueling fire they gradually succumbed. Two of their lifeboats were shot away, and it became the part of wisdom to abandon the ship before the other boats were destroyed.

Here was the German opportunity magnanimously to recognize a gallant foe after he had been vanquished. And the Prussians lost no time in doing it,—in their own happy manner. They circled raging about the lifeboats and fired into them with the utmost malice, killing two men and wounding seven. One of the murdered men was James Dawcy Fringer, a twenty-two-year-old boy from Roanoke, Virginia. The upper part of his person was shot wholly away; so that his bloody abdomen and legs remained sitting in the boat, and had to be pitched overboard.

You can see for yourself that these paladins of maritime chivalry do not propose to brook the gross affront of being fired upon by victims just because they are trying to kill the latter or force them into lonely open boats. They are quite clear, you can see, that when your enemy sets out to take your coach-and-four and valuables and leave you maimed and naked on the moors, if you try to resist him he has a right to shoot you dead into the bargain.

As has been stated, however, these cases are far from constituting the whole campaign, even against small ships; for there have been many very quietly conducted assaults, especially during the earlier stages of the war. All in all I should hazard the estimate that in one-half of all the attacks against the class of vessels now under discussion the guilt of the submarines has been confined solely to the abandonment of the lifeboats.

The ordinary course, when the submarine stops shelling upon the surrender of her quarry, is for the Germans to commandeer a lifeboat to send a boarding party to loot and bomb the ship. The boats are ordered alongside the submarine and a portion of their crews taken off. The remainder are then compelled to row a detail of submarine men back to the vessel. The boarders carry sacks, and often plunder the ship systematically, taking away tobacco and concentrated foods such as bacon, cocoa, and sugar. In most cases they appropriate the ship's nautical instruments. In a few cases, such as that of the *Solstad*, they have not disdained to pilfer the forecastle bunks, stealing the watches and small money from under the mattresses of the boys who rowed them aboard. Doubtless they feel that their compassionate abstention from shelling these particular victims is deserving of some trifling tangible recognition.

The bombs used are of various descriptions. An overside cubical bomb, with one face made very thin to be set against the hull of the vessel, has been several times reported. Since this type of bomb explodes two and one-half feet under water, with its entire force directed laterally into the ship, those who use it can stand on the deck and look down to see the effect when they touch it off. An American officer serving on a British freight ship was allowed in this way to detonate the three bombs, electrically wired together, which sent his ship to the bottom; and the Norwegian master of the *Storenes* had a similar experience.

Rather more common are the types of bomb designed to be planted in the ships' interiors, to be exploded by time-fuses. The bombing party can easily allow themselves opportunity to get clear of the ship before the explosions. These bombs are almost as poor in results as the shellfire; for very frequently the latter has to be invoked, along with torpedoes, to finish off ships which have already been bombed. I recall one staunch down-east American sailing ship, westward bound in ballast, which had two German bombs exploded in her empty hold without any apparent effect at all. The concussion appeared to squander itself impotently in the vacancy and against the stout Maine ship-timbers.

Lumber-laden sailing-ships, themselves constructed out of wood, proved by no means easy to sink; and the little pitch-pine carriers from our southern states must have been considered by the submarines as unmitigated nuisances. The fact that they never sought to escape or resist was more than offset by the prodigious floating capacity given them by their solid cargoes and well-lashed deck loads of timber. Sometimes the Germans tried the plan of shelling such ships at close range until they should heel over, then leaving them to be broken up by the action of the seas. Often, as in the case of the *Heathfield*, the boarding parties scatter inflammable oil or set incendiary bombs, and the ship may be seen burning for two or three days by the crew in their open boats.

I must not conclude the treatment of attacks upon unarmed and slow vessels without making the observation that no victim has been too humble or small o engage the attention of the submersibles. They had no false pride to prevent, for example, their destruction of the *John Hays Hammond*, a Grand Banks sailboat from Gloucester, Massachusetts, of less than one hundred tons register. This saucy little American craft came across the Atlantic under cargo, and lay for some days at Queenstown while the Consulate was adjusting a dispute between her owners and her complement. She intended to proceed from England to Iceland, and it was presumably on the bleak voyage to Reikjavic that she was snapped up by the omnivorous U-boats.

The attacks by submarines against fishing-boats have become notorious. During my stay at Queenstown, Germany was still trying to bolster up the fiction that she was "not at war with the Irish," and accordingly the submarines did not murder any Irish fishermen. Toward the last, however, they aid execute one brilliant action against the fishing fleet off old Baltimore in the County Cork, and their intrepid enterprise was crowned with a victory having a luster all its own. Eleven gasoline motors were destroyed, and the boat containing the leading fisherman was towed twelve miles out to sea and cast off at twilight with a single pair of oars.

Can you imagine an American naval officer carrying out a movement so loftily conceived! Later on, so the press informs us, the submarine raids against Irish fishers have become just as murderous as those against the English fleets working out of Lowestoft, Grimsby, and Yarmouth.

CHAPTER IV

SHIPS TORPEDOED WITHOUT WARNING

IN TAKING UP OUR SECOND GROUP OF SUBJECT-MATTER, THE ATTACKS upon freight steamers of fairly good size and speed, it may be said first and foremost that the larger the ships the more apt is the submarine to remain submerged and use a torpedo without warning. The Germans assert that they have been constrained into this policy because the better class of freighters carry guns. If they tried to give fair warning, they protest, their submarines would be fired upon and sunk by the very people for whose safety they were showing consideration.

This is a strong plea, with a compelling verisimilitude; for everyone knows that very many merchant ships do mount guns and are resolute to use them upon opportunity. In October, 1917, our Government declined to grant clearances to sailing-ships bound for the danger zone; and we may assume that slow ships are also kept out of the zone unless they are under convoy or are equipped with armament.

In assaying this contention for its percentage of genuineness, however, we are aided by turning to the numerous instances of submarine attack which occurred in the early days of the campaign.

In those days the freight ships had not yet commenced to carry guns, or were just commencing to carry them. Yet torpedoes were repeatedly used by the submarines without the faintest warning against ships which not only were unarmed but which the U-boats must have known or presumed to be unarmed. The most cursory glance at the evidence in the early cases shows this, and naturally many later cases can be cited.

To say nothing of the defenseless passenger ships which were sunk without warning-the *Lusitania, Arabic,* and others—we have the cases of the *Manchester Engineer, Storstad, Delamere, Cairnhill, Storenes* and *Hesperides*; and by a little digging I could give many more names of ships having no armament yet bushwhacked without forewarning. In each of these instances there were sufficient daylight and calmness of the sea so that the submarines could scrutinize their prey and note the absence of guns. It is a moral certainty that in a large proportion of these instances the submersibles had appraised their prospective "kills" before striking, and knew of the absence of weapons. Yet they deliberately elected to launch their missile in silence, a dagger-thrust in the backs of their victims. Why, even a rattlesnake sings before it strikes!

And even after the practice of mounting guns became more common, there have been cases just as significant in: showing the German determination not to warn unarmed ships. For such ships, namely, ships carrying no armament, have been torpedoed without warning under weather conditions so favorable that the submarines could easily note, and must have noted, the defenselessness of their targets. The Bromport freighter *Delamere* steaming between Goree-Dakar, West Africa, and Liverpool, laden with rubber and palm oil, carried neither gun nor wireless equipment. Yet she was torpedoed, in the spring of 1917, at eleven o'clock in the morning, one hundred and twenty miles from the Kerry coast, without a hint of premonition. She sank in: seven minutes, with a loss of ten lives. The steamship *Hesperides*, of two thousand one hundred and four tons, bringing maize from Buenos Aires, was not armed in any way. Yet she was torpedoed in fair weather at half past five o'clock in the evening last April without any forewarning whatsoever. She was two hundred miles west of the Fastnet at the time. The chief engineer was killed by the ensuing boiler explosion.

In both these cases, self-evidently, the iron sharks had all the opportunity in the world to study the situation before unleashing their death-bolts. In fact no special pains were needed, for the most ordinary care would have enabled the Germans to warn their quarry. In both cases, it may be said in passing, the submarines callously catechized the survivors in their open boats, and left them without any offer of aid.

The truth is that even at their best the submarines are never willing to take the least chance that their victims may escape. To use a homely and forcible Saxon phrase, these outlaws are so hell-bent upon driving through their successes that they will not even take the trouble to examine whether it is feasible for them to be humane about warnings. It is doubtless true that they have a wholesome fear of gunfire, but far stronger is the dread that they may miss some victim. It is not apprehensiveness lest they be fired upon which leads them to skulk up and assassinate a good ship in foul silence, so much as apprehensiveness lest that ship escape them if they give her any chance to get up speed. They have their choice of giving decent warning with the probability of getting their prey, or of not giving warning with the certainty of getting her. And the million-fold greater humanity of the first-named course has evidently no weight against the slightly increased effectiveness of the second. For the difference between probability and certainty they are ready to sacrifice any amount of human life! We may without pride, surely, be confident that an American submarine would take a chance on fighting fair, even at a little greater risk to itself and a slightly smaller chance of clutching an extra success.

Here is another angle: Devices for giving warning without exposing the submarine to counter-attack must be easily within the inventive capacity of the men who have perfected the modern German *Unterseeboot.* Even without any such special contrivances the submarines are able to play exasperatingly safe. Their periscopes barely emerge for a moment or two, the composition-glass lenses rising through the surface as dry as the palm of your hand. The observation is taken and the U-boat is safe back below before there is any rational chance of detection. We know—or can deduce it by ordinary common sense-that the great majority of the U-boats which are sunk are destroyed by war vessels or aeroplanes; for merchant ships can never, although frequently very gallant and efficient, take immediate advantage of transitory emergence by a submarine—unless their speed be doubled.

It therefore follows that the Germans could at small cost in danger or diminished efficiency institute ways of letting a freight ship know when they have got the drop on her; so as to give her the option, at least, of surrendering rather than be blown up. Smoke bombs could be used without emergence; or blank torpedoes, to strike with noise but not force, could be fired as a signal that other and deadly torpedoes would follow immediately unless the engines were stopped. Certainly means could be found if the will existed. But the Prussian naval gentlemen do not have the will. On the contrary they have from the outset seemed actually to prefer the fictional belief that all merchant ships are armed, and that armed merchant ships are always desperately dangerous.

If the Germans had originally put forward this armament excuse at a time when many freight ships really were carrying guns they would have had a strong case. But they were pumping this plea, with full tremolo effects of the "more-in-sorrow-than-wrath" variety, long before one merchantman in a half-dozen bore armament. The argument was an empty and impudent pretext at the time it was first fabricated to cloak a shark's-appetite for victims. The fact that circumstances have since changed to give it more color should not lead us astray. For the truth of the matter is that the Germans determined to sink any and every ship on sight, and to do their work free of any "sentimental" warnings which might embarrass the triumph of their cause. That truth is just as real today as it was three years ago. The presence of guns on board a freight ship is almost irrelevant and a matter of indifference so far as submarine success is concerned; but it makes a good dialectic point for expostulation.

In connection with this question of devising means of warning it should be noted that there has never been a glimmer of evidence that the Germans have even studied the problem. No one of the hundreds of ships which have been torpedoed has ever thought that she saw or heard anything which might be a German experimental device for warning. No stories have ever come out from Germany of inventors laboring to introduce humanizing devices for the submarine, either to give warning or otherwise. Would this have been true if America had been using submarines for three years?

I also urge that the German attitude as to warning either armed or unarmed ships be read in the light of their attitude on the cognate questions of shellfire, desertion of lifeboats, and the like. Courts of law take the general character of a culprit into consideration in passing upon his specific extenuating pleas.

If any reader still has a haunting misgiving to the effect that, "The Germans cannot be expected to jeopardize their own lives in order to spare the lives of others"—which is a mighty poor sentiment *per ipse*, so far as that is concerned—let him ponder those last two paragraphs well. I was recently informed reliably that the average educated man in Germany actually uses as an apology for submarines the statement that they are no worse than minefields; with the implication, first, that international law has sanctioned the use of mines against merchant ships, and second, that to the German mind there is nothing monstrous in such a use of mines. On the first point the fact is, of course, that mines have never been used indiscriminately in the open sea. The second point is highly interesting and pertinent for the ugly light it throws upon the German general state of mind. If any plan for slaughter can exist more insusceptible to being humanized or mitigated in its operations than the use of promiscuous mine-fields scattered casually about the open ocean, I defy any German sympathizer to name it. To say that the warningless use of torpedoes is no worse than mine-laying is like saying that murder is no worse than parricide. Let us examine how this German practice works out.

A fair hit by a torpedo is apt to sink a ship in remarkably short order. There are very many cases, it is true, in which the vessels float for quite a time; and it is these instances which yield the numerous anecdotes and the occasional photographs from which many people draw their impression of submarine attacks. Nevertheless such instances, if the Queenstown criteria are trustworthy, are the exceptions rather than the rule. I believe that at least one half of all ships struck by a torpedo without warning sink within the space of ten minutes or less.

A Cork packet-boat, the *City of Bandon*, torpedoed without warning at ten o'clock on a bleak winter night, sank in sixty seconds, with a loss of all but four out of her complement of thirty-two men. Her sister ship, the *Ardmore*, also torpedoed without warning, sank instantaneously, with a loss of all but one single member of her crew; and recent press dispatches state that two other Irish packets have been sunk without even a single survivor. The *Richard de Larrinaga* sank in three minutes, with the death of thirty-five out of her forty-eight occupants. Seven Americans died from this outrage. The *Lowwell* sank in one minute, and twenty-one out of her complement of thirty-one persons were drowned. The *Minnehaha* sank in six minutes, with forty-three deaths. The *Barnton* sank in thirty seconds, with fourteen men lost and nine saved. The American tank steamer *Montano* was torpedoed without warning on July 31, 1917, and sank in one minute, with a loss of twenty-four lives.

The first officer of the *Farnham*, with his arm in a sling, told me how his late vessel had been torpedoed in fair weather, with other ships close at hand, but had gone down so swiftly—in two minutes—that only eight out of her crew of twenty-three persons ever reached the surface of the seal The *Farnham* was an old ore-carrying tramp, homeward bound under cargo from Biserta, Spain. The torpedo and boiler explosions burst her hull clean in two amidships, so that the bow and stern folded toward one another like the blades of a jackknife. The sections rushed beneath the sea like lead; and carried down the hardy seamen like imprisoned vermin before they could even reach the decks.

A SINKING MERCHANTMAN FIRED BY TORPEDO.

This kind of cases could be adduced almost indefinitely, and the examples given are absolutely typical of a large section of the submarine victories. The merchant crews often work real miracles in saving themselves from ships which practically vanish beneath their feet, as in the cases of the *Karuma, Tela,* and *Thistleard.* But despite these cases, and the many cases in which the ship stays afloat for a considerable time, the general result of torpedoing a ship without notice is that she sinks so immediately that many of her occupants have not even a gambler's chance to save their lives.

If your adversary draws a revolver and fires it at you I suppose the chances are really only about one in three or four that his shot will kill you. He is more apt to miss you or to wound you. Yet jurisprudence maintains that your death would be a "natural and probable consequence" of his act, and he is held legally accountable pursuantly.

Now it is undeniable, even when every concession has been made, that the instant destruction of a victim-ship and her non-combatant crew is a "natural and probable consequence" of firing a torpedo without warning. So that no legal canons have ever been framed under which such an act, with *malitia praecogitata*, does not constitute plain murder, and murder in the first degree. And if the apologist points out that all war is murder, let him note that in civilized war the murder has never been planned and executed against inoffensive and helpless laboring men and civilians.

On the sea-floor at the bottom of the broad tract of sea known as the South Irish Channel there are lying several thousand corpses of murdered seamen; and if some of these poor fellows could be vouchsafed a few moments' resuscitation to come drip-ping into our Consulate with their stories we could know just what it means in murder to slip a death-bolt into a merchant steamer without warning. Short of that we shall never get direct testimony as to how the deaths transpire.

I cannot give, of course, details as to how these victims died. But our imaginations cannot lead us far wrong. We can see a group of deckhands or stokers, including farmer boys from Tennessee and pavement-bred boys from New Jersey, off watch in cramped forecastle, vigorously scrubbing their hands or laughing over a card-game or honestly snoring off the effects of their last meal of beef-heart or liver-and-onions. We can hear a sudden explosion and see the lights go out. The poor chaps start up with excited oaths and dash madly down a passage to a companion-way. Half-way up the ladder-stairs their leaders are sluiced back by a deluge of black sea-water. Scrambling and strangling in a heap, a few of these boys manage to get a foot on the ladder again. One of them, with his face taut in that fierce smile which is among our instinc-tive reactions to danger, forces his way, lifting one leaden foot after another, almost to the hatch. He is thinking clearly just how he will seize the hatchway and free himself to shoot upward to the face of the sea. And then, just while his purpose is most lucid, his face undergoes a curious relaxation, and his leaden feet cease to bother his mind any more. In another instant he is sliding quietly back among the quiet huddle at the foot of the companion-way; and presently he and his comrades have found, by the swirling of the water, that last posture, doubled upon the steel floor or slumped wisely into the corner of a door, in which they are spend-, ing the rest of the interval between the Great German War and God's eternity. Somewhere between them and the surface are the corpses of their bunk-mates Billy and Slim and Charlie Jackson. Billy had had a wild piston-rod driven through his skull; Slim was pinned into the scuppers by a rolling oil-barrel; and Charlie Jackson broke both his forearms when the after yard swung to port, so of course he couldn't swim but a minute or two. * * * * Back home in Dubuque or East Orange a mother finds herself sitting bolt upright in her bed, from a nightmare about one of her boys.

For the dangers attendant upon warningless torpedoing are by no means confined to actual drowning from the sudden engulf-ment of the ship. In at least one case out of every three, to begin with, there occur boiler explosions. If the submarine makes good shooting the torpedo strikes amidships and induces an engine ex-plosion with fatalities more horrifying than those from shellfire. I saw the magnificent Scotch chief engineer of the *Salmo* frightfully scalded about the head and torso; and when I left Queenstown he was said to be dying in agony at the Civil Hospital there. In a score or more of cases I listened to the most sickening stoke-hold stories of how brave men, frequently Americans, were blown into ribbons or boiled to death in live steam from bursting pipes. In the *Gafsa* case seven men were killed in the engine-room, and in the case of the *Camara* nine men were annihilated by the explosions. Similar death records, some greater and some less, resulted from the cases of the *Turino, Folia, Norwegian, San Urbana, Marina, Feltria, Snowdon Range, Cymric, Gibraltar* and *Memnon*.

These boiler explosions, contrary to a fallacy current among seamen, are not caused by the sudden immersion of the hot boilers in the cold water of the sea; for this contact has only a tendency to reduce the steam pressure. They are caused either directly by the concussion of the torpedo or its explosion, or indirectly by mechanical vagaries of machinery dislocated by the torpedo explosions.

A typical case is that of the *Vedamore*, a Johnson freight liner which was torpedoed without warning under a setting senescent moon just before dawn in a heavy sea in February, 1917. She sank in five minutes with a loss of twenty-five lives out of fifty-seven. The boilers exploded and wiped out almost the entire engine-room watch. Between ten and thirteen Filipinos and two American negroes were dismembered and destroyed in a manner too revolting for the mind to dwell upon.

Parenthetically I must tell you the story of the single person who survived from the engine-room of the *Vedamore. He* was a grizzled little Filipino stoker named Balbino Batiansilo. The force of the explosion drove him upward through the deck, without a stitch of clothing, after most of the lifeboats had left the dangerous hulk. He swam about until he came upon a waterlogged boat, however; and remained in this boat, bailing occasionally with his hands, without food, water or clothing, in freezing weather, until after ten o'clock that night,—a matter of eighteen hours. And when the lion—hearted little man was brought in to me three days later by a brawny Irish police sergeant, he apologized with Oriental politeness because his voice was husky in answering my questions! I am one of those who hope that the American flag, on some basis or other, will float over the Philippine Archipelago for many centuries.

The Booth liner *Crispin*, inward bound from Newport News, Virginia, to Avonmouth, was torpedoed without warning while laboring in a heavy sea on a thick March night in 1917 between seven and eight o'clock. The impact of the torpedo induced a boiler explosion in which five men were horribly macerated and killed; and two of these, as well as we could establish, were Americans. The Furness-Withy steamship *Swanmore*, which cleared from Baltimore, Maryland, about the time the United States declared war, was torpedoed without warning at twilight when she had reached a position two hundred miles from the Bull Rock. There were eleven deaths, due in greater part to the boiler explosion which at once supervened. The absence of warning may have been revenge, it is true; for the *Swanmore* had managed to sink a submarine a little earlier in the afternoon.

Boiler explosions form only one among the many secondary dangers from torpedoes; for the effect of dispatching a torpedo against a ship can never be foreseen. The missile may, for example, strike squarely upon a transverse bulkhead-wall, and jar the whole hull from stem to stern, as it did in one of the cases I handled. Such a shock causes a proportion of actual injuries and minor accidents, and adds to the fearsomeness of the disaster. Then there was a British case, from which the survivors landed at Queenstown, in which the torpedoed ship careened rapidly over on its side and then turned turtle. Many of the occupants were drowned; but the master and a few hardy spirits crept over the ship's rail, so he told our Mr. Heraty, and "climbed east while the bottom rolled west" until they found themselves sitting upon the keelson, whence they were eventually rescued. Such cases emphasize the inhumanity of launching a torpedo at a ship whose occupants have received no intimation of their danger.

Peculiar perils arise when a victim-ship carries hazardous cargo. The *Lucilline*, a naphtha tank-ship bound from New York to Calais, was torpedoed without warning in a heavy swell forty miles out at sea at two o'clock in the morning in March, 1917. The crew stumbled on deck into dazzling moonlight broken by scudding black clouds, only to find themselves immediately stupefied and unmanned by the fumes from the riven naphtha tanks. They became incapable of handling correctly the falls to the lifeboats, and displayed every sort of ineptitude induced by the "gassing." Only one man died directly by asphyxiation—and one from the boiler explosion—but twelve more were crushed or drowned by accidents arising indisputably from their incapacity. While the Germans are hardly ever aware that any specific ship carries naphtha, they do know that many ships bearing volatile oils pass through the danger zone and are certain to be among their victims so long as no effort is made to ascertain the character of the ships assassinated.

Sometimes, naturally, these tankers are overhauled and boarded without any special injury beyond the setting of the crew adrift. In such cases the burning of the cargo, which the submarine causes to be ignited, makes a striking spectacle. The burning of the *Hektoria* was described to me as having been a memorable scene; and so was the burning of the *San Urbana*. The latter vessel was bound from Puerta, Mexico, to Thames Haven, and was of nearly four thousand tons register. She was torpedoed without warning in April, 1917, at a distance of one hundred and eighty miles from land; and four men were killed by the boiler explosion. The remainder of the crew gained their lifeboats in safety, and for two days and two nights were able to shape their course, they told me, by the pillar of cloud by day and the pillar of fire by night from their burning vessel.

At one period there was quite a succession of oil-carrying ships sunk rather close together both as to time and place, near the Irish coast. I was told by a gentleman serving in the Volunteer Coast Guard that the waves which crisped along the headland beaches were iridescent and opalescent from the film of oil which covered the ocean. It was even rumored that the oil injured the fishing industry for a time.

The use of repeated torpedoes to dispatch a sinking ship is not infrequent, and affords one more evidence of the utter disregard for life or death with which the submarines put through their attacks. Two torpedoes were used against very many ships; and three in several cases, including the *San Urbana* and the *Annapolis*. The *Terence*, which was struck at eleven o'clock at night one hundred and ninety-three miles southwest of the Fastnet, received no less than four torpedoes. But in this case we can happily add that the U-boat had good and bitter cause to respect her adversary, for the *Terence* had stood her off in three separate brushes during the preceding day. The Leyland horse-transport *Canadian*, hailing from Boston, was torpedoed without warning at eleven o'clock on a bright moonlight night in the spring of 1917; and three additional torpedoes were sent crashing into her at ten-minute intervals while she lay sending up rockets and getting her boats off. Any torpedo might have demolished a lifeboat and all its complement; and the fact that no casualties actually resulted cannot possibly be accounted unto the Teutons for righteousness. In the case of the *Falaba*, the reader is doubtless aware, a third torpedo launched by the submarine in broad daylight from within a few hundred yards did strike squarely beneath a crowded lifeboat, killing two-score or more passengers and seamen.

The warningless use of torpedoes, we must remember, is far more than simply a proof of ruthlessness. It is a categorical and insolent repudiation of the time-honored formula of the law of nations, that "the character and cargo of a ship must first be ascertained before she can be lawfully seized or destroyed," — a principle by which American diplomacy has consistently taken its stand.

© Copyright by International Film Service

TYPICAL DECK SCENE ON A TORPEDOED SHIP: THE *FALABA*.

It is abundantly clear that in nineteen cases out of twenty, at least, the submarines know nothing whatever about the character of the ships which they sink without warning; except that from the size they can tell whether the victim is a passenger liner or not. Even when they are not in any fear of their quarry, and emerge freely for the use of gunfire, they never take the trouble to learn her nationality, cargo or destination before bombarding her. I recall only one case — that of the *Turino* — in which we had any respectable evidence that the U-boat was apprised in advance of the name and voyage of the ship they were attacking. Other cases have occurred, no doubt, but they are to the last degree exceptional;

and the Germans have taken pains to advertise them unduly with a view to inspiring an undeserved respect for the efficiency of their Intelligence Service.

This "hitting blind," without concern as to the nature of their victims, does not date merely from the 1st of February, 1917, when the unrestricted U-boat warfare was formally supposed to have commenced. As has been already explained, that date did not mark any real transition in tactics but only an admission no longer avoidable of a change which had already been gradually introduced. And certainly in so far as any pretense of learning the nature of a ship before destroying her is concerned, that feature of the campaign has been "unrestricted" from the very first day a submarine left Kiel. There is no need to furnish any list of ships attacked without knowledge of or reference to their character and cargo; for such a list would include nearly all the vessels which have been sunk.

The sowing of mines in the high seas is perhaps the practice which exhibits in purest form the utter contempt of the German selachians for the character of the vessels which they dispatch. We had two or three mine cases off Queenstown, outside territorial waters. I remember one in which five deaths were caused in the stoke-hold. A less tragic incident in this case was the wrecking of the galley, where a New England sea-cook saw his range rise up and fall asunder while he was himself blown off his feet. To name vessels as having been mined instead of torpedoed might constitute an admission that the Germans could turn to value; but the reader no doubt is conversant with some of the instances which have been officially announced. There was the passenger steamer *City of Athens*, for example, mined off South Africa in the summer of 1917, with the death of fifteen passengers. Five of the dead were Americans, and three of them were lady missionaries.

Before taking up the passenger attacks we ought to dwell for a moment upon the splendid heroism and capability which many armed merchant ships have displayed in fighting off their dangerous assailants. I have mentioned the cases of the *East Wales* and the *Swanmore*, in each of which two submarines figured, and in each of which one of the submarines was sunk before the gallant steamships were destroyed; and there must not be forgotten the case of the *Terence*, the maize ship from Buenos Aires which was attacked by torpedo twice and by shellfire at intervals for ten hours, and was only struck fatally late at night after her pursuers had for some hours not dared to approach her. One of the two torpedoes was a "dud," or defective, as has not infrequently been the case; and one was avoided by a very pretty steersman's trick after it had been sighted approaching the ship. Then there was the case of the *Roumanian Prince*, bound from Philadelphia to Plymouth with fuel oil, assailed by a U-boat in April, 1917. The submarine shelled the ship steadily for an hour from a distance outside the range of the *Roumanian Prince's* gun; and then retired, so that the plucky ship came clean away. And in the case of the *Gena*, reported by a consulate on the east coast of England, two German airplanes succeeded in bombing the ship fatally, but one of them was itself brought down by the ship's gun almost as the water was closing over the gun-crew.

It is only because the ships which make their escapes rarely happen to be bound to Queenstown, and rarely are questioned by any but Admiralty authorities, whatever their destination, that I have had so little to say about these "game" and successful encounters. Every week, as the official figures show, a goodly number of freight ships beat off submarines, and not infrequently sink them. Indeed whenever the encounter resolves itself into a running fight, with any speed at all on the part of the merchant-man, the U-boat is apt to be outdistanced.

There are very practical evidences that the British and American Naval authorities are not only proud of but satisfied with the efficiency of armed merchant ships against submersibles. One evidence is that special types of merchant ships are not being constructed for the emergency fleets. Freight ships might be constructed, of course, to lie low along the water, without superstructures and with internal combustion engines, so that they could slip through the danger zones and hardly ever be sighted. The fact that recourse has not been had to this type shows how excellently the ordinary merchant ships are felt to have acquitted themselves. The keen eyes, stout hearts, and ready judgment of our mariners and gun crews call for more appreciation than many of us, doubtless, have realized.

CHAPTER V

ATTACKS ON PASSENGER SHIPS

THIS BRINGS US TO THE THIRD CLASS OF SUBMARINE ATTACKS, THE most dumfounding, the most saddening, of all. We have seen that the submarines murder people who have made surrender, and that they kill from behind without a qualm as to the character of their prey. But I suppose the ultimate proof and manifestation of shark-nature lies in the attacks upon passenger vessels. President Wilson's epigram, that while property can be paid for, lives can never be paid for, applies with even stronger force in the case of passenger non-combatants than of seamen noncombatants. But more than this, the assaults upon passenger ships constitute war upon women and children-there is no other phrase for it-a course which since the invention of movable type has been unknown among the Caucasian races.

For a parallel to the *Lusitania* horror, as we knew it at the Queenstown Consulate, the mind gropes hopelessly through the events of recorded history. The Cawnpore Massacre in India in the Mutiny days is perhaps the most horrid crime which ever preceded the destruction of the *Lusitania*; but it was perpetrated by a people with infinitely less pretenses to civilization than the Germans. The Armenian and other unspeakable outrages in the Near East are likewise the work of a race impervious to western standards. Of course catastrophes like the Halifax explosion or Galveston flood, where the moral element is entirely absent, cannot be named in the same breath with the German attacks upon our mothers, our wives our sisters and our young children.

Many persons are ready to condone rough practice in warfare between man and man. They carry their belief that all is fair in war to such a point that when men are fighting and one side begins foul play they dismiss the development by according to the other side the right to work reprisals in kind. But I believe that no man reared in our western world, at least has ever gone so far as to apply such a train of thought to actions involving the gentler half of our race, the loyal and tender ministrants who mean so much in this peculiar existence of ours on the planet Earth. So that when the Germans descend beneath the seventh circle which any attacks at all upon women must constitute—when they aggravate a crime already execrable by denying any warning or any precautions for life-saving to such victims—I do not personally see how we can escape, while the heavens continue to arch above us, from de-nouncing this abysmal conduct as the consummate quintessence of depravity!

The Germans themselves even seem to recognize tacitly the quality of their deeds in passenger attacks; for I know of only one such attack, out of a large number, in which the U-boats have had the hardihood to hail and converse with the lifeboats from a pas-senger ship. On this point the miserable creatures have not quite raised themselves "beyond good and evil," apparently, for they have enough moral cowardice to shrink from facing passenger-folk whose nearest relatives they have just done to death.

The first passenger ship attacked after the *Lusitania* was the *Arabic*, a popular White Star liner sunk off Queenstown on August 19, 1915, with a death-toll of forty-seven persons. And let me state immediately, and insist upon the point, that neither in the case of the *Arabic* nor in any other passenger case whatsoever or wheresoever has there been the faintest forewarning on the part of the submarine. At least my information and belief are strongly m that effect. The U-boats have at various times had the grace to give warning to every kind of freight vessel; but they have never permitted themselves to give any notice of assaults impending upon ships carrying ladies and children! The German reason probably is that passenger ships are so speedy that to warn them would be to lose them; so that this attitude affords yet another proof that human life has no significance to the *squalidae* when it impedes German naval "glory."

The *Arabic* sank within nine minutes after being hit, and the limited casualty list is due solely to the superb self-control of all concerned. "Isn't it odd," said a Queenstown shipping agent to me, "how these big fellows go down like rocks almost as soon as the torpedoes touch them, while the little tupenny-ha'-penny tramps will flounder along quite comfortably with two or three torpedoes in their interiors?" This observation that passenger ships are the quickest to sink upon being torpedoed is a commonplace wherever the submarine campaign extends. Certainly there are many instances to support it. The *Lusitania* sank in eighteen minutes, the *Arabic* in nine, the *California* in ten, and the *Minnehaha* in six, as already stated. Nevertheless I think the generalization is a little too sweeping. The sudden foundering of a large ship impresses the imagination more than the disappearance of a small one; but the number of *augenblicklich* sinkings even among ordinary small merchantmen is very great.

The *Arabic* case brought out the grimmest instance of Manichean irony against an unfortunate mortal which has come to my notice. An American business man and his mother were homeward bound on the *Arabic*; and as he chanced to have a penchant for pedigreed dogs, he was taking out a pair of English bulldogs to exhibit at the New York Dog Show. When the *Arabic* was struck he conducted ills mother to a lifeboat and left her in the charge of friends and officers. Then he went below to save his dogs. Ten hours later when he came down the gangplank at Queenstown, with his dogs under his arms, he learned that his mother had been lost! Add that to your data on the "Problem of Evil."

The plight of the living, indeed, in these passenger cases always stimulated more pity than did the plight of the dead. The survivors rather than the corpses wrought upon our instincts. A man with a crushed limb is pathetic, but a man who has lost a little child is beyond conception more touching, we thought.

It was hardly more than a fortnight after the *Arabic* visitation before we had the *Hesperian* survivors on our hands. The *Hesperian* was torpedoed without warning, like the *Arabic*; and, like the *Arabic* she was outward bound from the United Kingdom. The torpedo struck her at a little before eight-thirty in the evening, in fair weather, on September 4, 1915. It must not escape our attention that neither of these two vessels was taking munitions to England, or even contraband food or stores. They were quitting British shores, and virtually all that they carried was a little assemblage of inoffensive human beings. Yet these empty ships were torpedoed relentlessly at the cost of many lives. It seemed incredible at the time. It seemed as though there were necessarily some error. Not until many months had passed, and instance after instance had befallen of assassinating empty outbound vessels, did we really grasp that this base practice had been from the outset part of a set policy. The duties which a raider or blockader owes its victims equally under human and divine law the Germans had simply spat upon and stamped upon.

As I look back upon the summer of 1915 it seems to me that almost the only progress which I personally made toward comprehending the truth about the submarine campaign was an awakening and a deepening of distrust about the German "explanations" as to any given attack. The Berlin foreign secretary, for example, alleged with egregious solemnity that the German commander who had sunk the *Arabic* believed that that vessel was attempting to ram his submarine. With regard to the *Hesperian*, similarly, Count Bernstorff seems to have been instructed to assert that she had been struck by a mine, not by a torpedo; and perhaps to add informally, with rare logical felicity, that anyhow the *Hesperian* carried troops.

The officers of the submarine which sank the *Arabia* must have been gifted with extraordinary judgment as to what constitutes an attempt to ram a submarine, for their alleged fright was inspired by a ship more than one and one-half miles away from them. The submersible in this case was engaged in sinking the freighter *Dunsley*, which it had attacked at quarter past six in the morning, when the *Arabic* appeared from the east at a quarter to nine, proceeding on a course parallel with the coast-line at least one and one-half miles further out to sea than the *Dunsley*. The submarine concealed itself near or behind the sinking *Dunsley*, with the hope that the *Arabic* might approach to give aid. The *Arabic*, however, did nothing of the kind; partly because the *Dunsley's* distress was not very plain at that distance, and partly because British ships had been instructed not to go near any vessel under attack by a submarine. The *Arabic*, zigzagging in a gentle two-point zigzag, held calmly to its course, which gradually brought it abreast of the *Dunsley* at a distance of nearly two miles. The submarine was disappointed to see the *Arabic* bear straight on, farther and farther away from it; and when the *Arabic* was two and one-half points past the *Dunsley* the submarine unleashed its torpedo. The passenger ship must have been fully two miles from the submarine at the time; and even if twenty minutes earlier some tack of her zigzag had brought her bow for a moment in the general direction of the U-boat the latter could not reasonably have had any apprehensions of attack at the time the torpedo was discharged.

The undertaking to explain the *Hesperian* outrage as due to a mine-explosion was even less plausible. The claim that the mine was an English one, or in other words that the British navy was using mines along its own coast, was of course simply laughable, merely from the standpoint of *a priori* reasoning, the Germans' own special forte. But the allegation that the explosion was caused by a mine at all met very promptly with disproof of the most solid and concrete kind. For the torpedo which sank the *Hesperian*, as has occurred in other cases, left large fragments of its casing in and upon the ship; and before she sank several of these had been picked up and taken into the lifeboats. Captain Main, F.R.G.S., is by way of being a bit of a scientist, and it was with scientific care that he preserved these torpedo-shards. They were examined with scrupulous care, not only by British experts but by American official experts at a time when America was trying to be neutral even in thought; and the fact that they are pieces of a German torpedo and not of a mine is absolutely past any dispute.

The supererogatory suggestion that the *Hesperian* carried troops was equally grotesque. Among her passengers were some thirty or more unorganized wounded Canadians, belonging to all varieties of military units. They were returning home as incapacitated, and had purchased their tickets individually at different times. Troopship, i' faith! The *Hesperian* was a troopship to about the same degree as the *Lusitania* had been a British Naval vessel; and I trust you have not forgotten that the Germans had the intolerable gall to excuse the *Lusitania* massacre by denominating that reserve ship a British Auxiliary Naval cruiser.

As I see it now the Berlin diplomats must simply have had a contemptuous faith in the credulous and confiding charitableness of the *blödsinige* Yankees. There really was not one legal scintilla of verity in the German "explanations" of the *Arabic* and *Hesperian* crimes. As for the precious evidence, or so called evidence, which the Germans fabricated to support their excuses in these cases, it is pretty clear that the German submarine officers willfully and carefully perjured their immortal souls for the sake of German destiny—willing to be damned for the glory of their Jehovah, as it were.

These two cases, at least, had the effect of teaching our Consulate that however one may gasp at German fabricated pretexts, such pretexts cannot be simply denounced offhand as arrant mendacities. In every case it is necessary to place on record proper and formal legal testimony about each minutest detail. For it has never been possible to foresee or conjecture just what part of the e-vents would be made the point of departure for German extenuating claims. Instead of roundly branding these claims as being palpable falsehoods we found that we must patiently proceed to accumulate a great weight of evidence to hang about Germany's neck, like the Albatross about the neck of the Ancient Mariner, at once the symbol and the proof of guilt.

Eventually the excuse-mill at Berlin slackened and ceased its operations, the inner degeneration there having reached a stage where the Wilhelmstrasse was actually unable to distinguish which acts it was expected to be ashamed of. Swollen pride at German victories, and gnawing irritation because those victories were proving to be apples of Sodom, carried Berlin to a pitch such that it no longer thought of making apologies or lying excuses to appease American sentiment. And thus in the fullness of time there came the *Laconia* case, which stands, so far as I am aware, without the shadow of a defense—a raw and flagitious crime whose perpetrators seem dead to any stirrings of honor or dishonor.

The fine Cunarder, whose destruction is not so familiar a story as it should be, was torpedoed on February 25, 1917, in rather boisterous weather, at half-past ten o'clock at night, without the faintest intimation by way of warning. She sounded her siren continuously, fired off rockets, and took a stiff list to starboard almost from the moment she was struck. The port side of the ship thus sloped outward, and in the initial confusion several attempts were made to lower boats down this projecting side; and sad to say No. 8 lifeboat was actually so lowered.

Isolated in its plight, this boat racked and rasped its way down the port side; and being a clinker-built boat, it reached the water leaking like a basket. It filled with water instantly, but was buoyed up by the air-tanks under its thwarts; and with its nineteen occupants drifted away, through the chilling drizzle of rain which presently began to fall, coasting the giddy twelve-foot ocean swells in the black darkness. I dare say that there are German apologists who would demand whether this estimate as to the wave-depth is an authoritative one, and who would reprehend any meteorological statements not based on readings of the barometer, the thermometer, or the wind-gage. Fortunately, while data of just that sort are not available, we do have abundant evidence of a somewhat different sort which will demonstrate whether the weather and waves were dangerous.

At half-past twelve in the morning, two hours after No. 8 boat set out on its grisly voyage, an English business man from Manchester, who had been sitting in tile bow, very quietly and uncomplainingly collapsed from exposure and fatigue; and before his neighbors recognized the situation he lay a lifeless heap in the sloshing water. As the night wore on two American ladies near the center of the boat found it necessary to stand continuously on their feet, so deep had settled the water-logged boat. Even as they stood the icy water swirled about their waists. These ladies were Mrs. Mary Hoy, of Chicago, and her daughter, Miss Elizabeth Hoy. They were originally Spokane people, I understand. They were proceeding to London to join Mrs. Hoy's husband and son.

At half-past one o'clock gentle gray-haired Mrs. Hoy sank down and tucked her head back like a tired child, and entered into the last sleep. After this Miss Elizabeth Hoy's mind seemed to be unhinged, so Father Dunstan Sargent and others deposed. She kept chafing the hands of the stiffening remains of her mother, and pouring endearments into those deaf ears, until an hour later a merciful heaven released her overtaxed spirit in its turn.

And one by one throughout the night the cold fingers of Death touched these innocent people on the shoulder—claiming even a stalwart American negro, Tom Coffey—until when the wan dawn suffused the winter sea the eleven survivors found themselves ship-mates with eight staring corpses. It had become necessary to free the laboring boat from all dispensable encumbrances, and in the pallid half-light of the ocean mists before daybreak the sprawling bodies were one by one slid overboard and committed to the sea.

Germany's destiny, we suppose, was thus brought a step nearer fulfillment. The submarine commander who sank the *Laconia* proved the one exception to my statement that the Germans shrink from confronting passenger victims. He showed no embarrassment in bringing his vessel alongside a lifeboat and demanding particulars as to the voyage, name, tonnage, and so forth. And he was surprised and manifestly pleased to learn what a prize he had drawn. Fearing that he had not heard aright, he exacted a repetition a second and third time, for his gratification, of the shocking information that he had without warning destroyed a passenger ship in the dead of a rough midwinter night. He then vouchsafed a remark that the British patrols would doubtless arrive in due time, and vanished without so much as a whisper cf inquiry as to the number of dead or the condition of the lifeboats.

For this exploit we cannot doubt that this denatured simulacrum of a man was honored by standing before Wilhelm II at Potsdam and having a decoration fastened upon his manly heart. Lieutenant Schwieger, who sank the *Lusitania*, we believe: received the Iron Cross of the first or highest grade, with the Order of the Black Eagle super-added to set the seal of Prussia's civilization upon that nauseous enormity.

I have not made an opportunity earlier to mention that the submarine which sank the *Laconia* was not content with a single torpedo. Twenty minutes after the first explosion it sent a second death-bolt leaping into the wounded ship, although by that time it could not fail to have seen that its victim carried passengers. The *Laconia* was brightly lighted to facilitate the taking to the boats. The submarine could see that there were people still on the decks, but was not by this deterred from firing the second torpedo.

The original explosion had taken place among bales of cotton; a fact which explains the slowness with which the vessel foundered,—nearly an hour. I have met Americans who, in their anxiety not to wrong the U-boats, were sufficiently soft-hearted and soft-headed to credit the submarine with having selected a part of the *Laconia* where the first torpedo would do slight damage, and with having then waited twenty minutes to give time for debarkation. The absurdity of this ascription, is glaring. The submarine had evidently no idea whatever as to the name of the ship she was assaulting, and could not possibly have aimed at a part of the hull specially capable of withstanding the stroke. The dark and misty weather, and the roughness of the sea, moreover, were such that no commander could have conceived or executed the finessing of a torpedo into a relatively safe section of the ship. The first torpedo was aimed to sink the ship.

The only deduction which the submarine could and probably did make before she fired her torpedo was that the victim was of liner size. The reader is doubtless aware that passenger liners average from two to five times as large as ordinary freighters, so that even on a dark night a single glimpse will often proclaim their character. The submarine which twice torpedoed the *Laconia* did not know what liner she was attacking, but probably had noted perfectly well that the ship was of liner magnitude.

The case of the *California* was of interest chiefly in supplying one more plain proof that the Germans have no hesitation in sending a passenger ship to the bottom without notice. The *California* was torpedoed in broad daylight under a clear sky at twenty minutes past nine on the morning of February 7, 1917. The explosion was muffled and deadened by the barrels of wax in which the torpedo struck; but it was none the less effective for its comparative quietness, since the *California* had completely disappeared within ten minutes.

The submarine in this instance must unquestionably have sized up the object of its attack accurately, and known her to be a fast passenger ship with a protective gun. The submarine's option then lay between attempting to give warning, which might or might not mean the escape of the ship, and torpedoing without warning, which was certain to mean considerable loss of innocent civilian life. Between these alternatives the U-boat did not hesitate. The taking or saving of non-combatant life has evidently no relevance in the selachian mind when the success of a ship-murder is in the scales.

After the torpedo had exploded in the *California*, the ship's engines could not be stopped or reversed, presumably because of flooding; and her momentum carried her forward at a pace which made the launching of the lifeboats hazardous, and thus accounted for the loss of the forty-one persons who were found to be permanently missing. The impossibility of stopping a vessel after a torpedo explosion has time and again played a deadly part in submarine tragedies. The classic instance, as you know, is that of the *Lusitania*, from which several hundred of the twelve hundred deaths occurred because of the vis *inertia* which carried the great leviathan headlong forward at just the critical juncture when the lifeboats should have been launched. The same thing happened in the cases of the *Abosso*, the *California*, and many other passenger and freight ships. The *California* actually forged ahead three-fourths of a mile in the brief space between when the first lifeboat and the last lifeboat quitted her. It may be said, on the whole, that in the average passenger case there is to be noted a queue or trail of lifeboats, many of them damaged, and of ejected and drowning passengers, strung out along the sea for anywhere from one to three miles behind the spot where the ship makes her last plunge.

Most often, perhaps, this inability to take the way of a big ship is due to the wrecking of the engines by boiler explosions such as have been already described. Or it may be due to the flooding of the engine-rooms, as in the case of the *Delamere*. In one case I heard unpleasant hints that an engineer had funked the danger of descending to deal with his engines, and that he was afterward conveniently drowned. In one or two cases, it was rumored, the masters cherished a fatal idea that by maintaining the speed of the ship they could keep the sea-water from pouring into the aperture as rapidly as if the ship were stopped. But in the main the heavy death-tolls arising from the momentum of the injured ships were due to causes beyond the remedy of the bravest or wisest of officers. I venture the estimate that one-third of all the loss of life in the submarine campaign—at least from passenger vessels—has resulted from the difficulty and delay which the ships' momentum or way has caused in launching the lifeboats.

Another passenger liner waylaid and sandbagged after her character had been apprehended was the Elder-Dempster ship *Abosso*, concerning which the American public appears to have heard very little. This fine vessel at the time of her destruction carried one hundred and twenty-six passengers, many of whom were the wives and children of British officials in West Africa. She was coming up from the Gold Coast laden with tin ore, cocoa, and palm oil; and was torpedoed with not a hint of warning at nine o'clock in the evening when three hundred miles off the southwest corner of Ireland. The engines were instantly put out of control by the explosion, and for a full half hour the gallant ship plunged hither and thither, yawing and veering erratically in her extremity like a stricken animal. A lovely sunset aftermath still lingered in the west, and a crescent moon and evening star were witnesses of the pitiful scene. Desperate attempts were made to fill and launch the lifeboats; but the anguished vessel repeatedly smashed and flung off the boats, spilling and strewing the sea with human beings like grains of dust. And when deep night closed down over those remote waters, out of the three hundred men and women and children who had struggled to save their lives nearly one hundred had become bits of inert flotsam on the long sea swells.

But the *Abosso* case is further significant, out of proportion to its mere numerical additions to the records of passenger out-rages, because it illustrates a German submarine practice of signal and esoteric baseness. The *Abosso* was one of those ships which the U-boats have deliberately followed during daylight hours and deliberately attacked upon the advent of dusk. Unbelievable as it seems, these poltroons have in many instances marked down their victims while it was light and slunk furtively behind them until night should descend to cloak the attacks. That is to say, they have selected for the moment of assault the time when their victims have the worst possible opportunities for self-preservation. In addition to the *Abosso* the Germans have used this vile strategy against the *Hesperian, Tritonian, Feltria, Crispin, Canadian, Ainsdale, Hesperides, Annapolis, Clan Macaulay, Galgorm Castle*; and doubtless many others. Who is it that the Scriptures say "love darkness rather than light"?

Just as in the case of so many infamous submarine practices, the idea that the submersibles were intentionally trailing their victims for hours in order to strike under the shadows of night crossed our minds at first only as an unthinkable suspicion. 'It very soon became a definitely non-ignorable hypothesis, and in the end a moral certainty. One proof was that the proportion of attacks occurring during the early part of the night, according to our Queenstown experience, became noticeably large. Another was the fact that in many cases ships were torpedoed in the evening in weather so misty and stormy that it was incredible they should have been sighted or picked up by the submarines except at an earlier hour. When a vessel is torpedoed on a dark night in moderately bad weather, despite her carrying no outboard lights — not even navigational lights — there exists a presumption of which any court of law would take cognizance that she has been reconnoitered during the day and tracked until darkness should shroud the death-stroke.

The Germans have their excuse, of course. They emphasize that the submarines can operate with more safety to themselves after nightfall. Like most excuses put forward by the inventors of poison-gas, this one possesses a *quantum* of validity absurdly incommensurate to the atrocity it is supposed to extenuate. The advantage in safety which the U-boats gain by deferring their attacks until nightfall is trivial in contrast with the increased peril to the non-combatant victims. Especially since the submarines have learned to do their work with high effectiveness without ever emerging is their recourse to the shades of night for security superfluous. The enhancing of their own safety is plainly only a minor object; and the principal object is to invoke the terror that walketh in darkness, to augment the number of fatalities. No cauldrons of moral guilt seem to outweigh to the Prussians any gain in their pet policy of *Furchtbarkeit*.

One more passenger case, to exemplify still another submarine characteristic, must not be omitted. The feature in this case is the U-boat hatred of wireless. Their fear of any radiographic communication amounts to an aberration. In the presence of wireless apparatus they behave with the same desperate nervousness which a woman shows in killing a snake. Of course when hostile war vessels are known or suspected to be within practicable range this violent antipathy to wireless is comprehensible; but the German interdiction is often enforced when there is not even a remote probability that the destroyers can come up in time to jeopardize German life or German success. So distant is the contingency of interference that the degree of German cowardice becomes too abject to be credited, and we suspect that the ban upon radio is due merely to a malicious intention that help shall never be forthcoming for the abandoned lifeboats.

The *Mantola* affair-and that phrase is almost pardonable in a case involving only seven deaths-is an excellent illustration. The *Mantola* was a British-India Line passenger boat outward bound from England for the. Cape and Calcutta, and was torpedoed in heavy weather without warning in the winter of 1917 when one hundred and eighty-five miles off the Fastnet. It so happened that although abandoned in haste the ship remained afloat for quite a time, and after her survivors had stood by in the lifeboats for an hour and a half the wireless operator and the chief engineer returned bravely on board to send off an S.O.S. call to bring help to the women and children.

But at the first click of the radio key the submarine, which had evidently been lurking on the murky horizon, picked up that message of distress and forthwith began a wicked bombardment of the derelict, so that the attempt to ask for rescue had to be abandoned. There was no rational chance that any Admiralty ship would be near enough to balk the submarine of its triumph, nor was there any other conceivable reason why that cry for succor should not have gone out across the sea. We are squarely faced with the raw dilemma of whether the submarine was simply the most Jaundiced super-craven ever extant or was black dastard enough actually to desire that those innocent people should perish on the sea without help!

CHAPTER VI

PERSONAL CONTACT BETWEEN SUBMARINE CREWS AND THEIR VICTIMS

OUR FOURTH CLASSIFICATION OF SUBMARINE ACTIONS DEALS WITH THE conduct of U-boat crews and officers toward the crews and officers and passengers from the ships destroyed. This demeanor ranges all the way from a maudlin and teary sympathy, through a shoddy brand of "Made-in-Germany" courtesy, to bluster and bullying, and finally to cruelties which would seem to be silly and puerile phantasmagoria were they not so revolting and so fatal. Perhaps it is a little ill-natured to stigmatize as cheap the kind of sympathy and courtesy that the submarine men do sometimes show; for the kinsmen of Hans Andersen undoubtedly must at times have genuine impulses of kindheartedness. But both sympathy and courtesy vaporize instantaneously whenever they seem likely to cost the Germans anything. As stated on a former page, I have never learned of any instance in which the submarine gave up any slightest advantage or put itself to the slightest substantial inconvenience for the sake of a humane act. Moreover the cases have shown that it is for the Teutons a natural and easy transition from the venting of cheap sympathy to the venting of cheap wit.

The crew of the *Oswald*, a steamer out of Pensacola which was sunk last April, were asked their destination by the submarine officers. Their minds reverting to their vanished ship, they said, "We're bound for Liverpool." The German officers exclaimed, "What a pity!" and then, "We wish you a pleasant voyage!" It was two hundred and fifty miles to the nearest land! The affidavit which I have before me states, rather woodenly, that this jibe was made "sarcastically."

In the case of the *Heathfield* the U-boat commander, with ready jocularity, leered at the survivors in the tiny shallop of a lifeboat with the injunction, "Take good care of yourselves!" The steamship *Castilian* was sunk by a submarine in half a gale of wind, two hundred miles from land, on April 18, 1917; and the supermen stood by in Olympian humor watching the struggles of the survivors, in fact openly laughing and jeering at them, so the witnesses swore. The *Terence* was destroyed late at night in the same month as the *Castilian*. The submarine held the *Terence's* lifeboats in parley to get the facts it wished, and then gave the curt and casual command, "All right. Now clear out!" The lifeboat had one hundred and ninety-three miles to traverse if it was to reach the land.

The master's boat from the *Delamere* was kept alongside the submarine with a gun trained on it for a considerable time, and then released with the command, "Now pick up your mates. Hurry!" Ten of the "mates" perished, and the boat could certainly have saved several of them. The U-boat could not wait five minutes, even for life-saving, before getting the details as to its bag. The use of swash-buckling threats "in King Cambyses' vein" is frequent, and the brandishing of revolvers or training of guns upon the little open boats is almost universal. The Germans threatened to blow the lifeboats of the *Hathor* out of the water if the master's identity was not revealed; and made the same threat against the lifeboats of the *Kinross* in forcing them alongside the submarine in a sea which seemed certain to crush them against it like egg-shells. This forcing of boats alongside submarines in rough weather has often occurred; and sometimes, as in the case of the *Eagle Point*, insult is added to injury by taunting and provocative bearing on the part of the conquerors. There was a Scandinavian case, whose name I cannot locate, in which the master was given a polysyllabic cursing ending with "Schweinhund" because he inadvertently used the English language in speaking to the submarine commander.

This kind of gentle japing could be adduced *ad nauseam*. While perhaps it would be insignificant if taken alone, it has a lurid illuminating value if taken in connection with the concrete acts of the U-boats. And often, as we have seen, it is hard to say just when these insubstantial injuries mount into the plane of substantial phenomena. In the case of the *Jose de Larrinaga*, a cotton steamer hailing from Charleston, South Carolina, twelve men were drowned. The submarine hovered about the scene without making any motion to assist or even to inquire about casualties. Indeed her officers actually took photographs of that death-scene to send to their fond friends at home! A similar callousness in the interests of amateur photography was shown in the case of the *Polham Hall*, and in at least two or three others. The artists in charge of the submarines divert themselves with their hobby in entire unconcern as to the lives of their photographic "subjects."

In discussing the way lifeboats are treated, however, the case of the *Cairnhill* stands out preeminent. This freighter of over three thousand tons register was bound from New York to Havre with a general cargo; and at eight-thirty in the morning, not long before America entered the war, her chief officer sighted a torpedo which approached from the starboard beam and passed astern. No warning had been received. You will perhaps be shocked to hear that the *Cairnhill*, upon this attempt to knife her in the back, proceeded in a very headstrong manner to get up increased steam, instead of waiting for more of the kind of "visit and search" the submarine was about to administer. The *Cairnhill's* speed rose from ten and one-half knots to twelve knots. As soon as the submarine realized this violation by its victim of international law it emerged, four miles astern, and betook itself to overhauling the *Cairnhill*, firing from time to time. Within another twenty minutes it was within half a mile of its prey, shelling the defenseless ship steadily. Two men on the *Cairnhill* were by this time wounded, and the starboard lifeboat had been carried away. It was necessary for fourteen men to crowd into the captain's gig, and twenty into the port boat. Among the latter were five Americans. The wind at this juncture was westerly, with a Beaufort velocity of No. 4, or ranging between fresh and strong. The surface was a northwesterly wave action, about No. 5 on the sea-scale, popularly described as rough and choppy.

The U-boat immediately came up to the boats and commandeered the large one, placing the occupants on its own deck forward of the conning tower, and taking the mate a prisoner below into its interior. Then the submarine's crew, under regular supervision by officers, entered the lifeboat and deliberately threw overboard the food, the water, the sails, and even the bandana handkerchiefs full of the little treasures the poor sailors were seeking to save. To put a point upon this hideous jest they actually filled the sweet-water cask with salt sea-water! The description called before me involuntarily, as I heard it, the loathsome tomfoolery of a troop of playful orang-outangs.

While engaged in bombing the *Cairnhill*, after making the master a prisoner, the Germans sighted smoke on the sky-line and rightly conjectured that a destroyer was in the vicinity. After setting their bombs, which they took time to do carefully and effectively, they returned to the submarine and went below with angry brusqueness. No sooner could they close the hatch than the submarine abruptly submerged, with not a hint of warning, leaving the nineteen men from her deck struggling in a cross sea one hundred and fifty miles from land with that gutted lifeboat for their refuge! So swiftly did the U-boat sink that these victims had not even time to dive off from the submerging hull. It was in the highest degree probable that the majority of them might drown; but by energy, heroism and luck at the end of thirty minutes the last man was pulled into the boat.

At the time the *Cairnhill's* lifeboat was originally gutted, please remember, the submarine had no idea that any rescue ship could be expected; and even when the warship showed on the horizon there was no mortal need for haste in submerging, as is shown by the deliberation with which the Germans continued to arrange their bombs.

The facts in this case were sworn to before me by five native-born American seafaring-men of excellent type, including the ship's boatswain, the carpenter and the cook. I know their story to be the naked truth and nothing else.

It has been our personal contact with cases such as this which has given me the capacity to credit the incredible *Belgian Prince* facts, as to which I have seen the evidence taken by one of the ablest gentlemen who has ever held the title of American Consul. The reader no doubt has read the circumstances in the press. The *Belgian Prince*, outward bound in ballast to Newport News, Virginia, was torpedoed without warning at half past eight on an evening in July, 1917, when two hundred miles west of Ireland. After the ship had foundered the submarine placed her complement of forty-four men on board its own whale-backed deck; forcing them to take off and throw away their lifebelts. It then proceeded away from the scene of the attack, covering a distance estimated at some fourteen miles. By this time dusk was gathering, even in that northern latitude; and the submarine plunged suddenly beneath the surface—with what thoughts in the hearts of her officers God alone knows—and left the devoted men of the *Belgian Prince* to die.

Well might the Germans believe that this rank crime would remain *spurlos* and unknown, with the silent heavens as its only witnesses. But the event was to be otherwise. At least three of the victims had shown the presence of mind to conceal deftly their life-belts under their coats when herded onto the submarine. I say "at least" three because there may have been others who died in the sea during the night. But at all events when morning came—fortunately it was midsummer weather—there remained three men borne up on the ocean maintaining feebly a precarious spark of life; and a vessel passed close enough to see them and rescue them.

Out of the forty-one men who died four were our fellow-countrymen. Of the three men who survived one was an unknown Russian, one was a twenty-three-year-old Virginia negro named Willie Snell, who had been second cook on the lost ship, and the third was the chief engineer of the *Belgian Prince* a man of some attainments and of indisputable probity. In the light of other German U-boat perpetrations I personally feel justified in considering this horrible occurrence as well substantiated as any sincere person could ask.

I will even go one step farther and mention a case which I have on hearsay only, from a merchant officer. This gentleman assured me that a submarine was definitely known to have captured a steward and his wife and put them through a "third degree" examination for information on the submarine's deck. When they proved intractably loyal and silent the Germans submerged suddenly and left them to their fate in the water. In consideration of its circumstantiality, and of the otherwise proven nature of the *genus squalus* in dealing with woman-hood, this story met spontaneous acceptance in my mind, and I still believe it.

Paymaster Hughes, of the British Navy, has been cited as authority for the recent case in which the crew of a captured German submarine tried to leave British prisoners, bound and gagged, on board to drown when her captors left her.

Since death sentences, with mischievous refinements, are executed light-heartedly by the U-boats, it is not marvelous that they should also resort to imprisonment of unoffending civilians. Beginning in the summer of 1916, it has become common for the submarine to make inquisition for the leading officers of each ship sunk. Such officers are then taken forcibly on board the submarine, and disappear from civilized ken. Their disposal is left by the Germans to conjecture, because the act is supposed to strike the other merchant officers into a palsy of fear. But even if their treatment consists merely in sharing the hospitality extended to other prisoners in Germany it is hardly a fate to be idly courted.

The instances in which masters and mates and engineers have thus been taken as hostages are very numerous; and to the best of my knowledge and belief the officers of the following ships, among others, have suffered capture: *Thurso, Lynfield, Saxonian, Penhale, Neath, Belgian Prince, Rowanmore, Harpagus, Tungstan, Baycraig, Hathor, Wallace, Eptalofos, Palm Leaf, Parkgate* and *Tremorva.* Captain Bullock, of the late horse-transport *Canadian,* is believed voluntarily to have sacrificed his life, by remaining on his bridge when the ship sank, rather than to fall alive into the maws of the steel selachians. Another master dove overboard, with quite a theatric effect, to escape capture; but the act proved unnecessary. The Germans in his case were apparently not thinking of hostages; and he was picked up safely by one of his own lifeboats.

In two separate instances, which may best remain unnamed, merchant officers have testified to having seen, while temporary captives below decks on German submarines, as many as four or five fellow officers of Allied nationality held as prisoners. There was a ghastly report strongly current at Queenstown, too, that a suffocated German U-boat had been raised by the Admiralty from the bottom of an Irish cove and had been found to contain, among others, the bodies of five drowned British masters. True or not, such tales emphasize the stolid and obdurate courage of the British mariners, who continue to sail through the danger zone without ever a sign of fear or even a tacit claim of heroism.

The objects for this practice of hostage-taking, resurrected by the Prussians from the murk of the Dark Ages, are threefold. In the first place it is supposed to enhance the submarine's immunity from attack; because to sink the submarine afterward must entail killing British subjects held captive on board it. Secondly, as indicated, it is designed to shake and demoralize the seafaring-men who are relied upon by the Allies to take ships in and out past the U-boats. Thirdly, it has been adopted because it does actually deplete to some extent the ranks of skilled navigators and engineers available to Germany's foes. The first and second objects have not been accomplished in the faintest degree. The submarines are as sternly hunted as ever, and the seamen of England, France, Norway, Italy and America pursue their calling without a trace of demoralization. Even the third object has given only minimal results, in proportion to the vast numbers of trained merchant officers in the merchant fleets of the Allies.

This retrogressive practice of taking hostages at sea, of course, has had its counterpart on land m the dragonnade of mayors and prominent men in Flanders, France and Poland.

CHAPTER VII

LIFEBOATS DESERTED AT SEA

NOW WHEN THE LAST SHOT HAS BEEN FIRED IN A SUBMARINE OUTRAGE, or when the assassinated ship has been swallowed up in the sea, and when the last coarse taunt, or malicious trick, or crime of capture or murder is finished—in other words, when the Germans finally quit the scene—where are the surviving victims left What end do the Germans design for them?

They are left tossing in fragile open boats, the sport of the ocean and gale, two hundred or three hundred or even four hundred miles out upon the face of the most cruel body of water in the world, the North Atlantic Ocean. The neutral elements of wind and sea, ready equally to serve or to injure humanity, are made the involuntary but horrible accomplices of the supermen.

Let me ask if you have recently been at sea in a bad storm? To the reader who has never lived continuously with or upon the ocean it is doubtful if any words can convey the awfulness of the struggle which a lifeboat faces when deserted to the mercy of the deep. But if you can turn your mind's eye back to a recent voyage, and call up the endless vistas of heaving waters and the soulless storms which battered against your ship when the elements unchained themselves, then you will be ready to put yourself in the place of submarine survivors, chilled and despairing, striving in pigmy desperation against the wild might of the Atlantic. You will be ready, too, to catch the full meaning of the abandonment of lifeboats by the Germans, and to adjudge the profundity of their sin.

Frequently not a single lifeboat ever makes the land to tell the tale of loss. A bit of floating wreckage, or an overdue notice posted at Lloyd's in London, remains forever the only evidence of the felony. Then again, as in the case of the *Highland Monarch*, cited by Alfred Noyes, only one survivor out of an entire crew rejoins humanity with his terrible story. In the case of the *Vienna*, which took place after I left Queenstown, five spectral and chattering Chinese were landed as the sole remnant from a ship's complement of over thirty souls. I understand that no coherent account of the assault has ever been procured. A ship's officer was still alive in the boat with the Chinamen when they met with rescue; but his extreme prostration not being recognized, he was allowed to fall into the water, and had not strength left to grasp the lifebuoy thrown to him.

It may be laid down as the most moderate possible statement from the facts—indeed as an understatement—that German submarines have never abstained from attacking a ship because of weather conditions imperiling the occupants. They proceed with subhuman imperturbability to put through their so-called duty irrespective of whether the lifeboats will be left on a tranquil sea or in a midnight whirlwind. The proportion of attacks made during tempestuous weather to the total number of attacks is at least in even ratio with the proportion of such weather to the weather in general. The assaults are made with the grimmest indifference to inclemency which promises death for the crews of the victim-ships.

The big barque *Inverlyon* was attacked by the Teutons in a sea so high that the port lifeboats could not be launched at all; and the men stepped from the ship's deck directly into the two starboard boats as the latter were swung upward on the foaming wavecrests. Only one of the *Inverlyon's* boats ever reached the land. The

Rowanmore was subjected to a scorching gunfire, and her crew thus coerced into the lifeboats, in October, 1916, during a storm so violent that the wave-troughs ranged from fifteen to twenty feet in depth. The master was taken hostage at the point of a revolver. The *Rowanmore* was unarmed; but fortunately she carried radio equipment, and was able to use it to bring prompt assistance. The British barque *Ravenhill* was bombarded viciously fifty miles out at sea in wild April weather. Only one lifeboat could be launched. Its occupants struggled with the hurricane for forty hours, and were then saved. The *Ainsdale* was attacked at a distance of one hundred and eighty miles from land in a tempest so bitter that although the lifeboat was adrift only ten hours two of its men were stark dead from exposure before help arrived. In the case of the *Cyrene* nine men died of exposure out of twelve after eighteen hours in a waterlogged boat. The storm in which the American oil-tank ship *Vacuum* was sunk was so severe as to kill eleven out of fourteen occupants of one boat in only eighteen hours of exposure.

The fine freight-ship *Feltria* was struck by a torpedo without warning under terrific weather conditions just before dusk in the spring of 1917, and sank in ten minutes; with four deaths from the boiler explosion. The land was only ten miles distant, but in that tempestuous sea it might as well have been ten thousand. The lifeboats congregated together for mutual aid and comfort as the night descended. Throughout the hours of darkness the long Atlantic combers charged ever and again through that little cluster of cockle-shells, occasionally flipping one lightly over; until when daylight came only twenty men remained alive on the scene. The original crew had numbered seventy-three! The submarine had talked with one of the boats before leaving them, expressing regret; and had aided a swimming officer to gain a lifeboat. This is one of the boasted cases of courtesy. The courtesy did not prevent fifty-three men from being slain by those who were courteous. Such sporadic acts of good-heartedness as have appeared in the submarine wastes of crime strike me, I am frank to say, like freak rose blossoms blowing in December, sterile and unfragrant reminders of a summer sadly done and gone. Whether generations must be plowed under before the German roses of warm-heartedness can bloom again we cannot know.

© Copyright by the International Film Service, Inc.

OPEN BOATS.

The *Galgorm Castle*, a big maize sailing-ship from the Argentine, was shelled by a submarine in February, 1917, seventy-four miles southwest of Bull Rock, just as night was falling. The shelling ceased when the lifeboats got clear. The weather consisted of a heavy sea, breaking, a misty rain, intense cold, and a southwest gale so strong that it had been driving the heavy and deep-laden old craft along at nine knots per hour. At the first shot of the submarine the *Galgorm Castle* clewed up its mainsail and cut the halyards to its topgallant. The U-boat could not possibly have failed to note these actions or failed to interpret them as surrender. Yet it maintained its shellfire so virulently that the crew tumbled into the lifeboats in that howling storm without daring to take time to stock them with provisions. The master's boat had its rudder broken in the exigent haste, and had to put off into the tempest in that condition.

The results were only precisely one-half as bad as was to be anticipated; that is to say only one of the boats perished. The master's boat was saved on the following day, and two fine American young men were among its occupants. They told me that Captain Frampton, the seventy-two-year-old skipper, and his wife who accompanied him, were both ardent Methodists; and that they not only labored with coolness and heroism but also lifted up their voices in prayer very fervently and audibly throughout that night of wrack and stress. The fact that the mate's boat, although it had the advantage of good steering-gear, was never heard from again, and must have been overwhelmed in the sea, makes the Captain's rescue a colorable instance of response to trust in Providence.

Two Americans were lost in the mate's boat. One was the runaway son of a New York business man, a boy of nineteen years, notable for his height of six feet and four inches. The other was a yellow negro from Stannardsville, Virginia, whose widow and little orphaned pickaninnies have the Prussian destiny to thank for their present condition. The death of the men in that boat ought to have been seen so that it might have been described. Just how their anxious faces confronted the blackness and bleakness of the storm, just how they relieved one another at bailing and steering, and one by one dropped down or were washed over and away, or how their boat never rose out of the cavernous hollow of some monster wave—all this we can imagine but not know. And the human beings who had willed and effectuated this horror, we suppose, had submerged after their evening's work into the calm levels below the storm to their evening's food and phonographs and sleep.

The cotton steamer *Towergate,* a little tramp coming up from the Gulf of Mexico,—I met her brokers at Galveston a few weeks ago,-was assailed by gunfire in rough weather at four o'clock on the afternoon of an April day in 1917; and under the stimulus of a couple of shrapnel shells near the boats the crew were able to get away in seven minutes. The submarine proceeded to destroy the *Towergate,* and then came up to the lifeboats, at about half-past five o'clock, apparently merely to give them a looking-over. Her conning tower was badly disguised with two small lug sails. She did not hail the boats. She left them alone on the ocean two hundred miles from land.

The two lifeboats naturally strove to keep together; but the weather frustrated the attempt, and by daybreak on the next morning, Tuesday, they had lost sight of one another. The mate's boat was never seen again, and must have been capsized or foundered with all hands. The fifteen occupants of the master's boat made a notable and noble fight for life. The violence of the storm mounted steadily through out the day, and during that night the boat staggered panting and tugging at a double-drag sea-anchor made of buckets. On Wednesday just before dawn the wind eased off. By eight o'clock they had the sail up and were lurching dizzily toward the land. Thursday morning was perilously rough again, and they gave themselves up for lost. But their bow rose to meet every billow, and late in the day the sea subsided. At nine o'clock that night, more than three days and three nights after their desertion, riding out the long black swells, they caught the glimmer of a lighthouse—the Blasquets Light—and with one accord lay down exhausted in the bottom of their boat. Morning found them still inert and powerless, broken by the long-drawn strain, although the land was within a dozen miles. It was two o'clock in the afternoon when by a kindly chance they were sighted and saved by a trading tug bound down from the north into Limerick.

I reached Limerick the next morning within an hour after they had awakened from the heavy sleep into which they had fallen upon their arrival. Five of them were Americans. I shall never forget their appearance o;r the appearance of their British comrades. Haggard, unshaven, with wasted cheeks and with dark circles under their eyes, their bones seemed starting through their unspeakably bedraggled clothing. They spoke in hoarse half-voices to tell me of their late companions. Some of the dead men, too, had been fellow-countrymen of ours, nourished by our sun and soil, and dowered with the fresh vigor of our western world. I wish that Scott Nearing or Mrs. Stokes could have taken my place at the oilcloth table where the testimony in the *Towergate* case was reduced into a written record.

At the risk of wearying you with these instances of exposure after submarine attack I must tell you of the *Marina*, an empty horse-transport westward bound to America, carrying to their homes a large contingent of American horse-attendants or "muleteers." The *Marina* was torpedoed without warning just before daybreak in the autumn of 1916; and the engine-room fatalities included two American coal-passers. Two of the lifeboats which got free from the foundering ship were manned almost wholly by our American boys; and for two days and a night, without proper clothing or sustenance, these tiny craft tore shore-ward together in a November hurricane. The vanishing of daylight on the second evening forty hours after the disaster, found them out of touch with each other, although not really far apart, driving at frightful speed before a roaring gale into the rockbound bay of Ballinskelligs, the most notoriously cruel of the dangerous Kerry fjords; and at nine o'clock and ten o'clock respectively they burned their last red flares, uselessly they supposed, in the mist and spindrift. Their doom seemed to have been seal d. I was reminded of Grotius' phrase, *"Inter fauces terrae."*

Meanwhile the ubiquitous and powerful forces of the British Navy had been at work. Tugs were beating back and forth across the path of drift from the disaster, and light-keepers had been warned by wireless to keep vigilant watch. The lookout at the Skelligs Light caught the gleam from those final flares, and signaled swiftly to a trawler; and before half-past ten the plucky little craft had rescued one boatload, and was steaming intrepidly into the depths of the bay in the pitchy darkness after the other.

And at eleven o'clock this second boatload was located at last, not four hundred yards from the raving surf-line under the cliffs; and the trawler drew alongside it. For a heart-breaking interval the help seemed to have come too late. Our boys were exhausted and chilled to such a degree that they could neither climb onto the tug nor even do their part in making fast to it. But instantly and indomitably the young British reserve lieutenant wheeled his ship about and thrust her boldly in between the boat and the nearing breakers, so that the force of the wind clamped the light lifeboat against her side while the eighteen Americans were lifted bodily like children by the British tars out from the very jaws of an awful death!

All honor, say I, to the fearless and tireless British Navy. Night and day, year in and year out, it has been keeping its wonderful resources steadily bearing against the German iron sharks. Britain's pride in the seamen and her Navy has been a thousand times well won by acts of hardihood and devotion which shed credit upon the entire family of mankind. And now, too, it has become possible for us as Americans to join our own splendid and stout-hearted destroyer crews under this encomium, for their brilliant and patient heroism in the most nerve-proving task ever set an American naval force.

As one who has been privileged to see both Navies at work in the danger zone I am proud to believe that never have brothers-in-arms been better paired in meeting labor and danger than are now the personnels of the Navies of the two great English-speaking nations.

The fortunate ending of the *Marina* case, how ever, was not matched in the case of another horse-transport, the *Russian.* The Leyland liner *Russian,* on a westbound voyage, also, was torpedoed without warning just after night had come down over an angry sea far out from land in the Mediterranean a month later than the loss of the *Marina.* Under drenching torrents of rain and a sky quaking with electricity the launching of the *Russians* boats became a wild nightmare; and one of the boats was overturned and lost, with twenty-eight deaths. Seventeen Americans were among these dead.

Just as submarines never withhold their attacks to allow tempests to abate, so they never delay because of distance from the land. In many instances a little forbearance on the part of the U-boats would multiply many fold the chances of their victims for survival. But the principle patently is to attack upon sight,—except when waiting to strike at dusk,—irrespective of the distance to the shore. The *Hektoria* was attacked and sunk three hundred and fifty miles from land, the *Abosso* three hundred, the *Killarney* two hundred and twenty, and the *Hesperides, Swanmore* and *Towergate* more than two hundred. Indeed the list of ships destroyed two hundred miles from land, as is well known, could be greatly extended; and the stories of desperate struggles to reach safety indefinitely so.

Curiously enough the case occurring farthest out at sea which I handled did not result in any deaths. The diminutive American lumber schooner *Woodward Abrahams,* of New York, was attacked on an April evening in the North Atlantic four hundred and seven miles from the Kerry coast. Her crew of nine men were deserted in that position; and for two days and nights they bore southward in order to reach a more frequented path of shipping. Their energy was rewarded, and their danger apparently done, when they were picked up by another little pitch-pine carrier, the Norwegian barque *Anna Maria*. But this rescue proved to be only a respite. Two days later the *Anna Maria* in her turn was sighted by a submarine. The Germans signaled to e Norwegians to send a boat off, and when this was done gave the master five minutes in which to abandon ship. The master protested that he had another crew, already once submarined, on board; and as an, act of grace the U-boat extended the time-limit by an extra five minutes!

Captain Van Namee, our New York Dutch skipper, marshaled his men nonchalantly once more into the little lifeboat from his own lost ship, and set sail valiantly toward Ireland for a second time. The winds were favorable and the sea kind; and so great progress did the *Woodward Abrahams'* boat make that it was within fifty miles of the coast a day later when sighted and picked up by a British Naval ship. In due course the sturdy captain and his men came stamping and joking into the Consulate, without a scratch or an ill, just six days after they had been left to their fate more than four hundred miles out upon the ocean wastes.

Like a large number of other incidents in the submarine campaign, the case of the *Woodward Abrahams* exemplifies the truism, previously adverted to, that men can and will work wonders when their lives are at stake. In the case of the *Margam Abbey*, reported by my colleague at Cardiff, the survivors were forced to tear the shirts from their backs to caulk the gaping cracks which their boat sprang. In the case of the *Verdi* the men held their hands in the boat's plug-hole while fashioning a new plug in rough weather a hundred miles out at sea. Yet in many such cases the boats win safely to the shore.

The summer of 1918 has brought the ultimate proof of the German indifference to distance from land; for already four cases have been reported of vessels sunk and crews abandoned twelve hundred miles or more from land, the cases of the *Dwinsk, Chilier, Manx King* and *Marosa*.

The mere fortuitous fact of the survival of fellow-men abandoned at all hours, in all seasons and weathers, and at all distances from land possesses no exculpatory force as to the criminality of the abandonment. Such survivals are due to the pluck, luck, stamina and skill of the victims. Do you remember that amazing specimen of Central European diplomatic explanation which emanated from Vienna in one of the cases in which lifeboats had been overwhelmed and lost after a harrowing fight with the sea? The Austrians urbanely stated that the boats had been deserted by the submarine thirty miles from shore in fair weather, and that if stormy weather had unfortunately supervened before the boats could reach safety this consummation was not the fault, of the Royal and Imperial Austro-Hungarian Government. The storm was accidental, and the injuries were no one's fault—*si tegula cecederit*, as the civil law hath it!

In many cases I think we may concede that the malice shown by the submarine is passive rather than active. The submarine officers not infrequently perform with a mechanical impassiveness the tasks into which they have been drilled by coercion. But there are countless indications that this impersonal—nay, positively inorganic—stolidity cloaks ill-will oftener than not; and that in the general majority of instances there is positive rather than negative malice in the abandonments of the lifeboats. For example it would manifestly be easy for commanders of U-boats, without fracturing their duty, to keep slow steamers under surveillance for several hours during violent weather, so as to postpone the attack until the sea could give the victims at least a decent chance to get their boats away favorably. In many cases, too, when such a ship is sighted far out from land the Germans might follow her for a day or two until she attained some proximity to the shore. Frequently assistance could be given to the lifeboats in the way of supplies or provisions, and it would often be feasible to tow the lifeboats some distance on their way toward land.

The almost universal absence of any of these natural and obvious acts of good-will by the men who are the instruments of Germany's U-boat policy fastens upon these men an unmistakably active and positive personal malice and evil-will. In cases where the submarines deliberately invoke the darkness of night as an adjunct in their crimes the quality of this malice becomes blatant; but in every case of the abandonment of boats the Germans rely upon an equally active expectation that the awful forces of Nature will be their accessories after the fact. It is definitely their intention that their victims shall not survive; and whether in any given case the outcome be life or death we are forced to take the will for the deed. The desertion of lifeboats, irrespective of the result in individual instances, accordingly possesses, like gunfire and the warning-less use of torpedoes, every requisite legal element of willful murder. And while gunfire and torpedoes are only particularized murder, the consigning of lifeboats to the ocean is so essential a part of the use of submarines at all that it constitutes an astoundingly universalized or wholesale system of murder.

One of the clearest proofs in this connection is the common refusal by submarines to tow lifeboats, even under propitious circumstances. In the early days of the war this was otherwise, and the submersibles from time to time actually volunteered to give their victims a leg on the journey to land by towing the lifeboats. We at Queenstown had more or less to do with reporting at least three instances of this kind—the *Blenheim, Belford* and *Thor II*—and possibly one or two others. Occasionally this genuine. German kindness cropped up even toward the end of 1916 and the beginning of 1917. In sinking the American steamer *Leelanaw*, in 1916, the Germans seem to have exercised such humanity as was possible, it will be recalled; and actually towed the boats for fifty miles.

In general, however, as the war grew more bitter these instances grew more rare; and by the late summer of 1916 the requests for towage which the victims had learned to make were almost uniformly repulsed. Even in the early cases the least shadow of a reason sufficed to deter the submarines from any act of mercy; and by the end of 1916 the U-boats usually did not trouble even to vouchsafe any excuse. They rejected the appeals for towage with silent disdain or even with abusive contumely.

The case of the Norwegian steamer *Storstad* is in point. The *Storstad* was bearing grain from below the equator, in the direct employ of the Belgian Relief Commission; and her errand of charity was plainly marked all over her hull and sails. The great canvas globes of the Relief Commission hung at two of her mastheads. She called at Las Palmas, and waited there — presumably until her letters of assurance from the Germans arrived-up to the end of February, 1917. After another delay at Gibraltar the *Storstad* at last reached the danger zone early in March, and was within seventy miles of the Skelligs Light when the sharks finally got her.

The submarine appeared at ten o'clock in the morning about three miles off the starboard bow-beam and commenced firing, at one-minute intervals. As the sea was rough they were unable to hit their object, and after fifteen minutes desisted and drew closer up to the *Storstad*. After another fifteen minutes, during which the nature of the ship must have become clamorously apparent, the Germans discharged a torpedo which struck the port side of the *Storstad* and reduced her to a sinking condition. The three lifeboats were launched within ten minutes; and the submarine, which was by this time only four hundred yards from the ship, proceeded to parley with them for particulars about the prize. The master of the *Storstad*, after a few minutes' talk, requested to be towed toward the land, and found that the submarine officers, for the first time, were unable to catch his meaning. He repeated the request with the utmost clearness, and found that the Germans apparently did not hear his voice at all. As a third and last attempt he and his men made signs by means of their ropes, and forced the U-boat to observe these; but the supercilious and contemptuous attitude which had found expression in expletives not a moment ago was now expressing itself in malicious silence. The commander of the submersible had no notion of spoiling his effect. He drew off and betook himself to shell the *Storstad*, occasionally plumping a shell near the receding boats, either by design or carelessness.

I need not go into the details of the lifeboats' struggles. The March weather grew worse instead of better. Only one of the three lifeboats was ever saved, so far as we learned; and one of the officers among her occupants lay down and died upon the deck of the Admiralty sloop, within ten minutes of the rescue, from the familiar complaint of "Exhaustion and exposure."

Other cases in which towage was refused are those of the *Hesperides, Westlothian, George Pynman,* and *Richard De Larrinaga,* and I know not how many more—certainly several score. The *Hesperides'* lifeboat appeared to be, and was believed to be, in a sinking condition when the submarine sailed away from it; but grit and ingenuity, with an abatement of the sea, kept it afloat until help arrived. In the case of the *Solbakken,* reported by our Consular Agent at Bilbao, the submarine towed a lifeboat very humanely until one o'clock in the morning; and then, because the weather became tempestuous, sought safety for itself below the waves, casting off the little boat summarily to its mercy. Alfred Noyes is authority for an instance in which a U-boat granted towage for an hour or more, and then suddenly and capriciously submerged without warning and without freeing the tow-line. Only the victims' quickness and strength in whipping out knives and sawing through the stout rope saved them from being dragged below the surface of the ocean!

RESCUED SURVIVORS OF A SUBMARINE ATTACK ON BOARD AN AMERICAN DESTROYER.

CHAPTER VIII

GERMAN MOTIVES
AND MORALS

THE ONLY SAVING FEATURE AS TO TOWAGE AND DESERTION, BY A SAR-
donic paradox, is formed by certain willful lying which the
Germans do—lying about the distances to the land. They frequently understate deliberately the length of the journey which
the survivors must accomplish to reach green earth again. In the
case of the *Vanduara*, a four-roasted Norwegian barque fetching
dye-wood from Jamaica, the submarine officer informed the Norse
seamen that Ireland was just seventy miles distant when it was in
fact two hundred miles distant. In the case of the *Killarney—in*
which the submarine had placed its wireless masts abreast instead
of fore-and-aft, to make its apparent course at right angles with its
true one—the Germans estimated the distance to the Fastnet at
one hundred and twenty miles when it was actually more than
two hundred and twenty miles. Similar understatements, some of
which have unquestionably been intentional, have been several
times reported.

Usually the victims have made their own nautical computa-
tions, so that the U-boat falsehoods are rather fatuous; but as symp-
toms of compunction the understatements are worth noting. They

show that some of the wretched supermen still cringe from facing the indignation, even if it be perforce unspoken, of their victims. At least this is the explanation most to be preferred. That such mendacities should be born from the mere wish to mock and tantalize is less probable than that their makers dread to meet the eyes of men who know the full facts as to the extent of the submarine's wrongdoing.

So much for the means and methods of the German selachians; or, better, so much for description of the cardinal external features of their submarine war. In addition to these external features there exist a number of less overt offenses which might well have been taken up, and which must at least receive some transient allusion here.

For example, there are the attempts, sometimes successful we know, to corrupt sea-captains by German gold to sell their honor and betray their own ships. Sometimes this plan consists in having the masters actually place bombs, or connive at the secreting of bombs, on board their vessels; and sometimes the masters have only been asked to rendezvous with a submarine which should carry out the actual act of destruction. I handled one case in which a vessel cleared New York ostensibly without wireless, but set up an emergency apparatus while on the Atlantic. This vessel was destroyed when she entered the danger zone; and the inference is too broad to be overlooked. Whatever the mode adopted, this policy of bribery and subornation is more than equivalent to administering poison-gas to men's souls; and it extends and abuses to an insufferable degree that agency to which all nations resort within proper limits, the agency of espionage or secret service.

The trampling upon diplomatic obligations and promises, new and old alike, which the Germans have made a part of their submarine campaign need only be barely mentioned; for the duplicity and scorn of honesty shown in Berlin's negotiations regarding the undersea warfare are already a familiar reek in the nostrils of all intelligent men. The fact that the submarines never seek encounters with vessels of war, so that their operations have none of the redeeming heroic elements of combats between armed contestants, would doubtless carry no worm wood for men who are so devoid of sportsmanship as to have coined the remark, "You will always be fools and we will never be gentlemen"; but it will hardly appear devoid of significance to Americans. Last but not least, the offenses against Belgian Relief ships deserve far more emphasis than can be here accorded them; and the assaults against hospital ships will never, until the invention of radical new departures in human expression, receive the treatment which we would all like to see them get.

All these features, however—the corruption of captains, the negation of honor in diplomacy, the avoidance of armed adversaries, and the destruction of food for orphans and of the lives of wounded men—must be dismissed with only a bare reference in this present account of visible and overt acts and deeds. The really salient concrete elements of the campaign are the bombardments, the stealthy use of torpedoes, the passenger attacks, the deadly mischievousness with which survivors are treated on the scenes of the disasters, and the invoking of the cruelties of Nature by abandoning lifeboats at sea. As to these latter elements the probative material has been marshaled in brief review; and having looked at the facts in regard to them, a further duty-and a very grave one—remains.

For from these tangible external phenomena, some of which lawyers call the autoptical evidence, our minds cannot fail to reason back to the kind of character which must lie behind them; and, from a consideration of the methods, to reach conclusions as to the spirit. In jurisprudence men's acts are held to be evidentiary of their states of mind; and in psychology acts are held to be the outward projections of inward "complexes" of mental, moral and emotional states.

There are some people whose nature is so kindly or idealistic that they shrink from their duty of appraising the German submarine guilt. They do not wish to see that when any unprecedented acts take on a certain degree of awfulness it becomes incumbent upon all men to give the best intelligence they can muster to a study, issuing if need be in a denunciation, of the bearing of such acts upon the great moral problems which humanity was created to work out. Presumptuous as it may seem for any man to pass a moral judgment, fate forces us to spend most of our time in doing so about every detail of life; and when we shirk this task the race fails to progress. Moreover such an adjudgment of the U-boats is a duty of patriotism; for no American can rightly support the President in this war unless he has formed personal opinions to the best of his ability about Germany's conduct.

At the Queenstown Consulate we could no more escape formulating opinions about the spirit of the submarine warfare than you yourself could avoid forming ideas about the character of any men whose behavior you are forced closely to watch.

In facing the ethical aspects of the German U-boat campaign the French and Italian and British publics have given America a splendid lead in the direction of fair-mindedness. They do not condemn the submarine blockade merely because it attempts to starve them; for they are attempting, with America's willing help, to starve the Central Powers. Neither do they condemn the Germans for having caught up and used vigorously a horrible new weapon of warfare, such as the submarine is. All war is conducted with horrible weapons; and the submarine, if used against armed combatants, has hardly more intrinsic horror than the poison-gas which, because we have been forced to; we are now ourselves using.

When gunpowder and other explosives were first introduced in Europe the piety and chivalry of the world execrated and denounced their barbarity and unfairness; and yet before many decades, on account of their miraculous efficiency, explosives were in use in holy wars just as they were in unholy ones. Undoubtedly, say our Allies, the time will come when other countries besides Germany and Austria will avail themselves of the frightfully effective instrument of destruction which the submarine has proved itself to be.

The gravamen of the charge against the German naval authorities, accordingly, must lie not so much in the fact of their having resorted to a subsea campaign as in the wrongful and perverted manner in which the new weapon has been exploited. For resolutely as the world has taken upon its conscience the use of explosives we have always recognized certain limitations. There has been a discrimination, more and more careful to the point of extreme scrupulousness, to exclude from the scope of destruction all persons not active participants in war. The use of living screens in battles has been prohibited; solicitous restrictions have been thrown around the besieging of inhabited cities. The rights of blockading or raiding warships against non-combatant ships have been closely circumscribed. (It is possible that the recent American and Allied air-raids against German cities form an exception; but these will be entered by the Recording Angel to balance the German air-raids, not the German submarine crimes.)

Thus on the basis of our past and present conduct, upon the whole, we may reasonably believe that the submarine in our hands will be principally confined to its proper use against vessels of war. We dare not say that its availability for use against non-combatant vessels—in other words its use as a blockader—will not be made the subject of continual experiment; but the inherent unsuitability of its employment on the high seas, because of the necessity of leaving lifeboats to the elements, will certainly result in restrictions similar to those heretofore worked out in such matters as the besieging of inhabited cities. President Wilson's high-minded words in this connection represent the whole Allied mind, "We shall, I feel confident, conduct our operations as belligerents without passion, and shall ourselves observe with proud punctilio the principles of right and fair play we profess to be fighting for." And this being true, it is a fair charge that the Germans have employed the new horror against an improper class of persons—civilian non-combatants.

But totally aside from, and more important than, the dubious quarter in which this new weapon has been applied, is the needlessly degraded spirit in which it has been applied; a spirit observable alike in its operations against proper and against improper objects of attack. For in using explosives, as is well known, the nations have not stopped with restricting the class of victims but have gone further and eliminated in every way possible the non-essential horrors, even in wars between armed combatants. Expanding bullets of the dum-dum type have been interdicted, as have poisoned shells; and every facility for assistance to the wounded has been safeguarded. Whenever it has been possible to mitigate the awfulnesses attendant on the use of explosives and other weapons this has been done. So that if ever, under stress of peril or temptation, the civilized powers should resort to the submarine for blockade work against non-combatants, we may at least assert, and assert with absolute vigor and positiveness, that we would strive to humanize and elevate its use to the utmost degree possible.

This is where the Germans have fallen so lamentably into the slough. So far from seeking to temper and soften the inherent horrors of submarine warfare they have deliberately sought to accentuate and augment them. They have willfully omitted and turned their backs upon the many measures that might so easily civilize without impairing the force of their weapon. Nay more, they have in many particulars maliciously added to its natural horrors and intensified its intrinsic barbarity. It is precisely in this uncalled-for and gratuitous aggravation of the cruelties native to submarine work that the German crime is most blinding and unbearable.

The substance of the crime being thus defined, we are immediately faced with the question of motivation. Have these excessive atrocities been the result of the official German will or have they been contributed spontaneously by individual commanders? And, whether the one or the other, have they been conceived calmly and scientifically or have they sprung from passion, hatred and personal cruelty? And again, if all these elements, official and personal, mental and emotional, enter in at various times and places, in what proportions do they occur? Which ones are paramount or predominant? Any answers which we can find to such questions as these cannot fail to affect our relations with and attitude toward not only Germany as a whole but individual Germans for very many years to come.

The fundamental answer, so it seemed to us at Queenstown as we toiled amid the evidence, is that by far the greater part of the U-boat wickednesses do flow from a single—and thank heaven a rather impersonal—source; but that the campaign was also stained by a shameful quantity of personal and emotional spite and cruelty. The great and omnipresent underlying principle which has caused the quality of the submarine blockade to repel humanity has been the official Prussian ruthlessness—and I wish there were a good unused synonym for that hackneyed word. The getting of results, without reek or ruth as to incidental means or consequences, has been the first and only consideration, it seemed to us, of the spiritual descendants of the "Man of blood and iron." Human life, individual or collective, has seemed to have lost not merely its sanctity but any consideration at all. And, as the greater includes the lesser, human suffering and the rights of womanhood and childhood are also ignored. The under-sea war, as Berlin has willed it, knows no alleviations, no mutual understandings, no humanizations. It is simply stark one hundred percent war.

This cold-blooded and calmly-reasoned governmental policy accounts directly—in broad outline at least—for many of the worst submarine atrocities, such as the attacks upon passenger ships and the abandonment of open boats. Individual commanders have no scope or responsibility on such actions. The decision has been immovably fixed by Berlin as a consequence of the official determination utterly to subordinate means to ends.

A touch of the personal does enter in, of course, even to this impersonal principle, in so far as it has been evolved by Junker statesmen who happen to be themselves peculiarly brutal men. It is at this point that we first must take cognizance of that strain of beastly personal cruelty which has long been a notorious characteristic of a certain class of Prussians. The presence of this racial defect in many of the men who create Germany's policies must have entered into the production of the otherwise impersonal ruthlessness.

But aside from this intrusion of a moral deformity which marks many individuals in Prussia the ruthlessness of the U-boat campaign is, as has been said, an abstract governmental policy; based on mental processes and ratiocination rather than on any existence in the German Government of actual malignancy or anger. It represents the German Government's reasoned conclusions as to the way in which submarine war should be conducted. If two countries are at war, says the German brain, the quickest and therefore best way to terminate that situation is to make the war as thorough and extreme as possible. All war consists in doing evil that good may come. Why not do enough evil to bring about the result at the earliest moment? Why do anything by halves? Many an American has been rather caught by this superficially rational and practical doctrine.

As a creation of academic logic this argument is possibly of classic flawlessness; but in ordinary life, fortunately, people do not act upon abstruse logic. They act upon individual virtues and vices—or likes and dislikes, if you prefer—modified to a reasonable degree by the results of brain-work. That is why as individuals we never find ourselves in private life conducting a one hundred percent feud with an enemy, no matter how he has wronged us. If a man injures me by economic competition, or steals my goods, violates my home, or attempts to murder me, I seek retribution it is true, and seek it energetically—Americans believe in taking their own part—but I do not declare a one hundred percent 'war upon him. I may boycott my enemy or sue him, or have a stand-up-and-knock-down to take the meanness out of his anatomy, or even in some contingencies get a gun and go after him and shoot him. But I do not kill innocent neighbors' children incidentally to my vengeance, nor do I arrange to have him die of thirst even if that be the only means of retaliation available. And I do not desecrate his corpse, burn his house and torture his widow as a warning to other men that I am not to be trifled with.

At least if I come from a civilized or semi-civilized race I do not do those things. And if I did do them I would be considered not merely a criminal but a maniac. The world recognizes that such acts, however rational they may be from the logical standpoint, are so far removed from true reasonableness that they are in fact the very acme of irrationality and insanity.

The situation as between nations is strictly analogous. Being aggregations of individuals, they behave in the same irrational but very human and rather convenient way that individuals behave. A nation which insists upon one hundred percent war is just as truly an international monster and maniac as a man who kills innocent third parties or wreaks savagery in a personal quarrel is a private monster and maniac. To justify submarine atrocities by saying that they are simply results of Germany's *durch-und-durch* logicality is a slander upon our God-given reason.

In each of America's wars there has been much of mutual forbearance. The War of 1812 was decidedly a good-natured one, with neither side very warmly roused against the other. During our Civil War there were endless instances of amenities and reciprocal respect. During the Spanish-American War neither side was bitterly inflamed; and I have no doubt there are Spanish incidents to balance Captain Phillip's remark off Santiago, "Don't cheer, boys; the poor fellows are dying!"

But clearly as we now see that the submarine ruthlessness, bred from the idea of making war a one hundred percent affair, is a colossal and wicked error, there was a time when we were willing to admit that this error might conceivably be a sincere one; and that it had a semblance of evil grandeur, like the designs of Milton's Satan in "Paradise Lost." Earnestly as we repudiate and revile it, there was once a feeling that if submarine atrocities are the creatures solely of this intellectual Frankenstein the heart of the German people might still be relatively unsullied. And for quite a time at Queenstown the evidence showed enough cases of German submarine courtesy almost to delude us into thinking that the German: crimes sprang from a brain-mistake due to the German worship of abstract mental processes.

There was one piece of evidence particularly which supported this view. An American merchant officer named Adolph Colstad, born in Norway, but for thirty years an American citizen, chanced to be serving in the autumn of 1916 as mate on board the late steamship *Harpalus*. The *Harpalus* was a collier bound from Bristol to Nantes, and was attacked at ten o'clock in the morning thirty-eight miles southwest of Galley Head, Ireland. For nearly three hours after the attack it befell that Mr. Colstad—I believe he holds an American master's license-remained in the company of the German officers of the submarine. Inevitably he struck up an acquaintance with them, and after a time even ventured to tax them for an explanation of the cruelties of the submarine campaign. To his astonishment they assured him, very earnestly and with tears in their eyes, that if they ever withheld their hands for the sake of showing mercy, and if their crew informed upon them on the return to Germany, they would be put to death officially by slow physical torture. They further stated that two different German submarine commanders have actually been tortured to death in the Fatherland for acts of compassion as to which their crews have "peached" upon them!

When Captain Colstad told me this I turned and said to him rather sharply, "Surely, you did not believe any such fantastic hoax as that?" "But I do, Mr. Frost," he insisted with dignity. "They made me believe it. I want you to put it in my affidavit." And he not only stood fast in his belief but eventually swore to it. Some courts would exclude this testimony under the Hearsay Rule, and some would not. It is submitted here for such weight as you care to give it. Personally I think there is at least a measure of truth behind it, and that many of the submarine officers believe that no mercy will be shown them by their Government if they permit any human weakness for mercy to interfere with success.

The evidence of Captain Colstad was too late and dubious, however, and the courtesy instances were too sparse and defective, to countervail the cases of disgusting and flagrant cruelty which had grown to be pretty frequent by the end of 1916—pure brutalities such as those of the *Ainsdale* and *Madura* and *Eavestone* cases. We could not but note that the courtesies were usually meretricious and cheap; and we were forced to conclude that while civilities are probably enjoined by the German Government the injunction must be neutralized by an understanding that the quality of mercy must be very scientifically strained. For whenever the Consulate would begin to feel, for a fortnight or so, that the impersonal ruthlessness at Berlin was the seat of all the blame and guilt we would suddenly again get little clusters—two or three cases—of the nauseating and aggressive barbarities for which mere ruthlessness could never account.

Even so there remains an alternative from supposing that these devilries arose out of native individual black-heartedness. They may be samples of terroristic *Schreclclichlceit*. For ruthlessness cannot stop with merely caring nothing about the lives of its victims. It is forced, if it is to be consistent, to extend itself into an active desire to terrorize its foes in the only way terror can be generated, viz. by actual death and cruelties. The official German injunction to ruthlessness has therefore presumably been supplemented by instructions to practice frightfulness whenever feasible. Just how this can be squared with the instructions about courtesy is hard to say; but I fancy that in both matters the instructions are not so much formal as informal, drawn from personal interviews and contact by commanders with their superiors, so that different ideas are uppermost at various times. General rules for acting like fiends can hardly be laid down; and it follows that no matter how spontaneous and intimately personal in origin a piece of dastardliness may seem, it may still represent an honest effort by a submarine commander to follow instructions from the men higher up.

The idea of frightfulness, as applied to submarine war, would of course be for each commander, when the circumstances seem to him right, to behave with such ferocity that the entire South Irish Channel and other infested waters will be shunned by every merchant seaman. Given a general idea such as this, and finding that the merchant seamen are strangely unwilling to be terrified, there are hardly any lengths to which a commander may not go in his flustered hopelessness of bogeyizing our staunch sailors. It is not improbable that some of the worst submarine cruelties have been frenzied attempts by commanders to put frightfulness across against men who do not seem even to know when they are frightened!

A GERMAN SUBMARINE SURRENDERING TO AN
AMERICAN DESTROYER.

But after all, whittle down the personal element as we might, there remained among the Queenstown cases a small irreducible residuum of cases whose facts showed flatly that the submarines' men took more than cordially to their work, and were improvising barbarities on mere casual temptation, owing to downright

Frederick-the-Great bloodthirstiness. While there might be no positive criteria for deciding whether given acts were conscientious attempts to terrify or were gratifications of innate private cruelty, still there would be strong indications toward the latter conclusion. There would be a lack of self-possession and self-control about the Germans which showed that they were quite beside themselves, and were incapable of acting solely to carry out a reasoned policy either of ruthlessness or frightfulness. Flushed faces, stuttering objurgations, and impromptu hectoring in ways that were almost as ridiculous as repellent—all these were signs that the U-boat men were simply giving free license to their tempers and were yielding to their wild-beast instincts. Most of these were Prussians, we supposed.

These volunteered-cruelty cases, thank heaven, do not form a very heavy percentage of the total. Averaging the campaign as a whole, my guess would be that up to eight percent of the attacks have manifested a heathenish love of cruelty for its own sake; and that perhaps an equal share have shown genuine, even if very incompletely obeyed, impulses toward kindness. What of it? In a campaign conducted by any of the civilized western powers the kindness-cases would include practically all, and there would certainly be no such percentage of red-Indian savageries. You do not say of a neighbor, "He is a good man, for only one out of twelve of his acts is mean and vile."

But even if it were possible to decide—for the above opinions are frankly only estimates—just how much of the campaign is due to collective and how much to individual wickedness, there would still be the question of why there is such wickedness at all. Conceding that the Prussian autocracy is a clique of metal-boweled Macchiavels, and that the average German is warped and wrought upon from the age of unresisting infancy until he can manage to worship any sort of national Baals, we have still to account for the evolutionary history of those autocratic anthropophagi and of the conditions under which human beings can be taught cheerfully to work abominations.

The most generally-accepted theory of explanation is that the form of government, with its pagan repression of th(l individual, has gradually evolved or permitted the evolution of the German moral degeneracy; and every true democrat must concur in ascribing great evil to this autocratic form of government. Another factor frequently emphasized as contributory to the shocking nature which Germany has revealed in the war is that strain of animal cruelty mentioned a moment ago as characteristic of some classes of Prussians; and unquestionably such a strain has played an important part in Germany's development. The autocracy must be abolished and the cruelty bled out. But I submit that there is a third factor just as important as either of them which has gone into the production of the war and of the submarine atrocities. This factor is continental overpopulation.

I do not mean overpopulation so much from the political as from the moral standpoint—overpopulation as it tends to produce cynicism and brutal-mindedness. No American who has lived in Europe can have failed to notice the heavy and over-breathed atmosphere caused from the presence of too much humanity in proportion to the landscape. The surplus-age of human beings has a triple effect,—it cheapens the value of each individual, it embitters young men by tautening economic competition, and it diminishes the amount of wild Nature available to each man for his re-creation. In Germany the heavy birth-rate and the population of three hundred and twenty-four people per square mile—in America we have about thirty—has certainly depressed and depreciated the respect in which each separate individual is held. The economic competition, likewise, is proverbially so constricting that each young man sees his career stretching ahead of him as inexorably as a pair of steel rails. If he does not keep to the way marked out for him by his circumstances and his superiors he must either emigrate or suffocate. And, lastly, the effect of familiarity or unfamiliarity with God's out-of-doors ought not to need stressing to Americans; and in Germany it is hardly possible to find any large sanctuary of Nature unexploited by beer-vending *Gasthäuser* or in some way besmirched by man. These are the influences which have generated, as much as any others, the cynicism and contempt for the finer things of life which some of the present-day Germans have shown; and their connection with the submarine apparition is immediate, not remote.

To the obvious comment that Germany is by no means the only overpopulated country in Europe must be collated the fact that her situation is peculiarly calculated to bring out the workings of what may be called the spiritual counterpart of the Malthusian Law of Overpopulation. England plows and reaps the seas, and her economic tension is relaxed by her vast accumulated wealth. France has only two hundred people per square mile; and the lowest population index of any of the great European countries has given her the highest spiritual index. Among the smaller countries the utter impracticality of "hacking a way out" exercised a chastening effect and prevented the ferment of aggression-conquest from ever starting. Thus Germany has been a special sufferer from the law—and it is far sounder than the Malthusian Law proper—that multiplying humanity cannot multiply spiritual foodstuffs indefinitely. And I am personally disposed to give the Germans credit for realizing that something of the sort was amiss, and for striving to remedy it by various economic expedients and by contriving to make their supplies of wild Nature go as far as possible. They fostered all kinds of excursions afield, and taught young people in the *Sturm-und-Grund* period to rhapsodize methodically about the beauties of forests and mountains. Unfortunately there are some things which cannot be forced even by Kultur's efficiency; and the wholesomeness that springs, as Americans have such good cause o know, from an abundance of resources of Nature is one of those things.

Just as the confining of people in an overcrowded room generates pulmonary diseases, or just as the confining of men on a ship without fresh acids generates scorbutic diseases, so the stifling population conditions in Germany have generated among some classes the spiritual diseases of cynicism and brutality. The Germans are from this standpoint to be regarded as the victims of a moral auto-intoxication or infection—a spiritual leprosy if you will—for which they are by no means solely to blame. Sternly as we are bound to stamp out the disease, we must take its causes into consideration in passing judgment upon the submarine campaign; and also, may it not be said, in reaching any final condition of world peace.

CHAPTER IX

SUMMARY AND APPRAISAL

AND NOW WE HAVE NOT ONLY EXAMINED, AS PLAINLY AS POSSIBLE, THE methods or concrete operations of the German iron sharks, but we have gone further and examined their spirit, as it was reflected by American witnesses at Queenstown. It may be well to recapitulate briefly the conclusions under both parts of the examination.

With regard to the methods or acts such a summary will furnish a definite set of counts to the indictment we projected at the outset, a sort of "J'accuse" or formal enumeration of the malefactions of the submarines of the Central Powers:

1. The German submersibles have repeatedly, almost systematically, shelled defenseless vessels after unmistakable surrender. If America ever uses submarines against merchant ships the shellfire will cease, it is safe to say, the moment it has produced surrender.

2. A peculiarly vindictive gunfire is reserved by the German U-boats for any vessels which make the slightest attempt at escape, although this escape is not from visit and search but from being cast adrift in frail lifeboats in the open ocean. An action so natural and justifiable as seeking safety will never be the pretext for splenetic savageries by submarines of civilized powers.

3. Still more bitter and cruel are the measures kept in store by the German sub-sea boats against victims who attempt to defend themselves by any armament. After attempts at resistance, and in some instances even after attempts at escape, there has been gunfire against little boats which had left their sinking ships. Here again no non-Germanic submarines will indulge in infra-human revenges for efforts toward self-preservation on the part of civilian seamen.

4. Against unarmed vessels the German use of the torpedo has habitually been without any warning, even under weather conditions rendering the observation of lack of armament so easy as to be absolutely obligatory. The least duty imposed by decency before the firing of a missile calculated to cause sudden destruction is to seek earnestly to discover absence of armament and to make human allowances accordingly.

5. Against armed merchant vessels no warning is given before the use of torpedoes, and no attention has ever been given by the Germans to the problem of how warning might become practicable. The U-boats have preferred to take the fact of armament as relieving them from any further human responsibility for the lives of their victims. The naval authorities of most nations would have made strong efforts to develop devices for giving an armed ship at least the option of surrender.

6. With malice prepense the German submersibles are regularly attacking passenger ships carrying innocent civilians of all ages and sexes. Such attacks will never be made by the naval vessels of any other people.

7. German submarines seldom offer assistance to survivors swimming in the sea, and they frequently insult and injure the occupants of lifeboats, on the scenes of the assaults. Much would

be done by ordinary submarines to aid survivors by lifesaving apparatus and by emergency rations to provision lifeboats.

8. German U-boats seize non-combatant captives to serve as hostages. This practice will probably be outlawed when international public sentiment can be again enforced.

9. The marking of a victim-ship during daylight and following it to strike after nightfall, to add to terror and death, is a feature of the German submarine tactics. Non-German submarines would probably reverse the process and defer attacks from darkness to daylight.

10. No forbearances are made by the Teutonic submarines because of stormy weather, and victims are therefore frequently subjected to needless perils from gales and wave-action. The contrary policy, with surveillance until tempests can moderate, would be easy of adoption with comparatively negligible loss of efficiency.

11. The German attacks are also made without reference to distance to the land, thus producing much gratuitous exposure and misery and death. American submarines, we need not fear to assert, would seek to follow the objects of their attacks until the shore was approached, so that the survivors might have better chances to save their lives.

12. Requests for towage toward land are usually refused by German submarine commanders, even when the conditions are propitious for towage. It is inconceivable that the craft of any other nation will ever be guilty of such refusals.

Here we have a round dozen of explicit and definite statements—arranged in logical rather than rhetorical order—for which the evidence has been briefed upon earlier pages. It is the evidence of honest and intelligent American citizens drawn from all walks of life, and of expert and responsible officers and engineers. In so far as taken at Queenstown it was recorded by a man of legal habit of mind, well-disposed toward the Germans, and of internationalist-pacifist tendencies; and in every case it has been taken by American officials selected and commissioned by the President and Senate of the United States.

The facts thus testified and recorded show forth, it is submitted, a Satan's carnival so shameful that it cannot be described even by the word "war," as that word is known to white men. The German sneer that, "War is not cricket," takes on, in the light of the submarine facts, an incredible hatefulness. War may be deadly without being dirty. And for Emperor William, with the gangrened corpses of thousands of innocent non-combatants before his mind's eye, to announce unctuously that he will triumph, "With God and my U-boats," is the most impious and profane blasphemy ever taken upon the lips of a human being!

Let us epitomize, in turn, the results of the brief inquiry undertaken as to the motivation of the German submarine campaign, namely, its moral aspect, remembering that in this case the summary is not so much an indictment as a diagnosis:

1.   The essence of the Teutonic guilt as to undersea warfare lies in the spirit of that warfare, and not in the mere exploitation of a new and terrible weapon of destruction. The fact of the submarine campaign, that it to say, is less odious than the manner of it.

2.   The general note of this spirit is an officially ruthless will to conquer at any cost, even at the cost of intentional atrocities to produce terror and dread.

3.   Supplementing the governmentally-prescribed ruthlessness and frightfulness, there have been occasional supererogatory volunteered brutalities. We need not regard these as typical of the German people; yet there seems little reason why they might not be so regarded.

4. The primary underlying cause of the official policies of pitilessness and terrorism has been the German infirmity for crude intellectualism-a servile submission to dehumanized *a priori* logic; and a secondary cause has been the presence among the despotic classes in Prussia of a long-demonstrated vicious relish and craving for physical cruelties.

5. The private and impulsive brutalities, together with the willingness of the individual Germans to execute the inhuman injunctions of their Government, are due to cynicism and callousness engendered partly from the form of the Government, partly from the pervading Prussian cruelty, and partly from the degradations inevitable where population is excessive. The Germans as individuals may be thought to be sound at heart, except where they have become victims of a hitherto little-recognized moral pathological condition.

It is no part of my province to discuss the strategical success or failure of the submarine campaign; a subject, for that matter, upon which any man can reason for himself from the officially published data. The weekly toll of ships sunk has remained about stationary for the past nine months, despite the advent of the American destroyer flotillas; and the British Chancellor of the Exchequer announced recently that the U-boat total of over six million tons sunk last year was offset by only two million tons of construction the world over. Our Treasury Department, by its insurance rates, estimates that one ship out of every twenty-five which go into the danger zone is destroyed; and Lloyd's Agency calculates that if five ships undertake transatlantic trade for a year one of them will be destroyed. The tonnage which the Chairman of the United States Shipping Board hopes may be built in America this year is only slightly over half of what the Germans sank last year; while our requirements for General Pershing are mounting convulsively. At a rigid estimate more than eighteen thousand innocent non-combatant men and women and children are now rotting beneath the sea from these shark-forays. These familiar facts are merely cited here in order that if the heinous cruelties discussed in this book have not aroused you against the submarine menace your interest may at least be shocked awake by impending national shame and danger.[*]

The facts about this appalling gehenna of brute crime and murder ring with an iron clangor of peremptory challenge. America and England are girding up their powers ever-increasingly m our shark-hunt royal, rejoicing as strong men rejoice to prove their mettle in the face of danger. For these selachian German monsters must and can be vanquished and overwhelmed and extirpated like the dragons hunted by the knights of Uther's son; and America, which grappled and subdued a stubborn wilderness, will find the riveter's hammer as true a weapon as the pioneer's ax, and will not relax a fiber until she has flooded the face of the sea with the hosts of ships to stifle and smother this equally inhuman adversary. Rancor and hatred the shark-outrages can never provoke in the hearts of true Americans; but grim resolution and high purposes they cannot fail to kindle fiercely. We must reiterate from our inmost beings the pledge voiced by Beatrice Barry—

"That little children may in safety ride

The strong clean waters of Thy splendid seas,

That Anti-Christ be no more glorified,

---

[*] These sentences were written in March, 1918; but at the present time of writing (July 25, 1918), while some of the facts have altered they still express my point of view. Several British officials have within a few days issued warnings against the wave of newspaper optimism; and the loss of the *San Diego*, the *Leasome Castle*, and the magnificent *Justicia* ought to carry the warning home into any serious mind. Pressimism about the campaign would be insanity, of course; but a sober and ever-vigilant spirit must be maintained yet for months, if not years, to come.

To mock Thy justice with his blasphemies,
We come; but not with threats or braggart boasts.
Hear us, Lord God of Hosts!"

THE CRIME OF THE
"LUSITANIA"

CHAPTER I

THE QUEENSTOWN BACKGROUND

I LANDED AT QUEENSTOWN, MY SECOND OFFICIAL STATION, ON MAY 14, 1914; about three months before the beginning of the war, or about a year before the *Lusitania* disaster. The landing was like an arrival into paradise. A rose-madder daybreak in the east and a pale-gold moon setting in the west threw an unneeded glamour over the romantic fortresses of Carlisle, Camden and Templebreedy, and over the estuaries and inlets of the most beautiful harbor in the world. The town of Queenstown, rising against the abrupt hillside of the Cove of Cork, in the clear morning light, was crowned by the Admiralty House and the fine spires of St. Colman's Cathedral. "The pleasant waters of the River Lee," celebrated in Father Prout's verses, spread, shimmering, before the prow of our landing-tender in positively Hesperian loveliness; and the massive rock escarpments under Spy Hill were gorgeous with purple valerian and golden laburnum.

This was the place which, little as we could then guess it, within a single turn of the seasons was to plunge into a species of waking-nightmare unimaginably trying. It was to give eternally compromising connotations to the word "Hesperian" by the

127

tragedies of the vessels *Hesperian* and *Hesperides*, and was to take the music out of Henry James' phrase, "Lusitanian loveliness." It was to be known no longer as the world's most stately harbor, but as "the port of horrors."

The background in which these horrors stand to me, that is, the preliminary events and consular activities, can be filled in in a few paragraphs. Queenstown proved to be a busy consular post. The inspection of emigrants, the invoicing of Irish whiskey, mackerel and tweeds, and the issuance of bills of health to the passenger liners-most of which still touched at the port-provided a substantial office routine; and a great deal of consular notarial and legal work arose from the fact that the South of Ireland is saturated with people who have American ties. Then there were the American tourists bent on visits to Killarney, Blarney, Glengariff and Cappoquin, and the Irish-Americans who had come on summer pilgrimages to the "ouhld sod."

And it so proved that when the early days of August brought the cataclysmic opening of world-war these tourists and trippers produced in the Consulate our first foretaste of war work. Tammany judges and policemen, ladies' maids and chauffeurs, clerics and liquor-vendors all poured in and out of the Consulate in quite a continuous stream; often merely to learn in what way the war was likely to affect their personal plans, and often to apply for gratuitous transportation or loans. Fortunately for us very few of these latter applicants could fairly claim to need financial aid, since they all possessed friends or relatives in Ireland from whom to borrow. We did loan money occasionally; a hundred pounds, for instance, to a stranded aggregation of Irish-American motion-picture artists who had been staging scenes in the Black Valley. But in the main our service lay in reassuring those who were over-timid and in impressing upon those who were overbold the importance of getting back to America at an early date. We sent many cable messages to friends and kindred in America, often through the medium of the Department of State.

One general service of considerable importance the Consulate was able to perform for these travelers. The British authorities toward the end of August reached a sudden decision to close Queenstown against the arrival and departure of all persons other than British subjects. This was in the highest degree natural, as Queenstown is both a naval and military center, but it meant that our throngs of Irish Americans would be forced to make an awkward detour to Liverpool before they could take ship for home. The Consulate suggested that really the most expeditious way to "sterilize" the Cork "fortified area," and the South of Ireland in general, of aliens would be to drain the latter off rapidly through Queenstown instead of retarding the outflow by deflecting it through Liverpool.

This viewpoint was presently adopted, after numerous official calls, and Queenstown was held open for embarkations until well into November. The number of residents of America who availed themselves of the privilege thus gained was about six thousand; and their saving in money alone, in avoiding the trip to Liverpool, must have been about seventy-five thousand dollars. I think this may fairly be cited as one of the numerous little instances which show the pecuniary value of our Consular Service to the American tax-payer.

In October, when the main rush of the exodus was dying down, a big passenger steamer bound for a neutral continental port was brought into the Queenstown road-stead and detained over a question of contraband. She carried a large and vigorous group of American saloon passengers, and these quickly became very restive. We got into communication with Ambassador Page by telegraph; and in the course of time the Ambassador effected an arrangement by which the voyage was permitted to continue. During the following week the incident bade fair to be precisely repeated; but in this ease permission was procured for the American and other neutral passengers to disembark at Queenstown and proceed by rail and packet-boat to London. We hurried about after nightfall and chartered a tender on which we steamed out into the choppy waters of the road-stead and brought ashore two dozen wind-blown but high-spirited Americans.

With the general discontinuance of travel by Americans the consular war work took on a different character; concerning itself with commercial opportunities, German interests, American freight ships, and intensive investigation of the claims of various persons to American citizenship.

Vast commercial opportunities were opened up in Ireland by the cutting off of trade with the continent. All kinds of hardware and enameled ware, glass and glassware, musical instruments, knitted goods, leather sundries and several other lines of merchandise had been coming into the Province of Munster—our consular district—from Germany, Belgium and Austria.

Of "German subjects and interests," too, the Consulate, like all our consular offices in Allied countries, had charge. Ireland, as is well known, was prior to the war filled with German waiters and hotel employees who reported—or misreported for the sake of pleasing their German overlords—the Irish political situation to Berlin. The larger share of these, I think, managed in one way or another to leave Ireland when the war came; but quite a few who did not do so applied to me for certificates as to the facts in their cases. These certificates, they hoped, would exonerate them from charges of "slacking" when the war ends. In cases of internment of Germans the British authorities, without any obligation to do so, were often so kind as to explain the situation to us; and in every case they could well afford to explain with the utmost candor, for their treatment of the Germans, while thorough, was certainly most generous. The matter of furnishing weekly financial relief to the dependents of interned Germans, out of funds lodged with Ambassador Page at London, involved no little consular investigation and correspondence.

The crews of German merchant ships captured by the British, and the German sailors taken from neutral ships, were landed from time to time in County Cork to be sent up to the internment camps at Tipperary and Oldcastle. It devolved upon us to collect the wages, and sometimes the effects, of these men, and forward them to the camps. Some of the German sailing vessels were owned and manned by the excellent type of Germans so familiar to Americans in America; and it was really pathetic to see them parting from their pet linnets and from the ship's cabins which they had spent years in converting into pleasant homes. I shall always have a high regard, for example, for Captain Immelman, of the German barque *Melpomeme*; and my wife was touched by the mounted specimen of the South American white heron which he left in a pasteboard box labeled "Qriosité present for Mrs. Frost"-whom he had never seen. He had originally acquired it to be a present for Frau Immelman back in the Fatherland.

It should be said that in all my rather extensive correspondence with these prisoners after they had reached the internment camps there was never an **int**imation of complaint as to the food, quarters or treatment which they were receiving; nor at the manner in which the camp Commandants administered the wage-funds or other funds of the Germans.

The war brought work of still another kind to the Consulate by attracting American ships into the transatlantic trade. In the old days, before the invention of wireless telegraphy, nearly all the ships approaching England with grain, timber, sugar, etc., had to call at Queenstown for orders as to their destination; and in those days—or at least during the early part of them—the American merchant marine was large enough so that many American ships entered the Cove of Cork. But with the introduction of wireless and the decline of American shipping, Queenstown ceased to be familiar with the American flag; and for more than nine years before the war the Stars and Stripes had not been flown by a merchant ship in the harbor. Accordingly we were rather glad when the high freight rates resulted in the occasional appearance of American vessels once more.

These ships, however, whatever their size or rig, almost always sought Queenstown because they were in trouble of some sort; and they claimed an amount of our attention disproportionately large. Two of them had been in collision, and two were worm-eaten old coasting schooners which never ought to have tempted the North Atlantic storms. In several cases there were altercations between the masters and the crews; and the La Follette seaman's law in the Consulate became well-thumbed. We tried to adjudicate uprightly about such matters as duff and pork; and once held a solemn cabin conclave concerning a little sheet-iron stove which had been bought at Brest to heat a draughty forecastle. The relations between the seamen and the local Constabulary, when the crews were accorded permission ashore, took a little watching. One American captain distinguished himself by several kinds of disgraceful conduct; and we visited the police court to hear him receive a richly deserved reprimand. Then there was the pleasanter case in which three Americans pluckily stayed by a tug-boat whose British officers and crew deserted her during a storm well out at sea. Our three men brought her safe to land in my district, and through our efforts and those of the Consulate-General received later a generous sum for salvage.

The most complex and trying work of all was the determination of American or non-American citizen-ship status. Prior to the war Americans never thought of taking out passports for visits to Ireland; but wartime exigencies and the fear among Irish Americans that England might enforce military conscription in Ireland made the establishment of national status supremely important. There are scores, if not hundreds, of persons in the Province of Munster who consider themselves Americans but who have as a matter of fact and law forfeited their American nationality. The Irish political troubles made the sifting out of these classes a pressing duty. Sometimes a young man's nationality depended really upon his preexisting state of mind, and it was necessary to try to ascertain what his actual intentions and ideas had been when war and rebellion had not been to the fore. Persuasion was brought to bear upon our judgment in these and other cases in the form of various proffered gifts such as bottles of whiskey, banknotes, umbrellas, inkstands, and kindred miscellany; and we could not note that the profferers had the faintest notion of any moral aspect to this species of *argumentum ad hominem.*

CHAPTER II

THE NEWS AND
THE PREPARATIONS

THESE WERE SOME OF THE WARTIME DEVELOPMENTS OF THE ROUTINE consular work; and while we were occupied with them a multitude of outside features began to bring home the realities of the war, and to suggest that further development which was to overshadow everything else in the Consulate for more than two years of my incumbency. The naval activities in Queenstown admonished us of strenuous days to follow, and the military changes were interesting, too. The casualty lists from Flanders began to strike here and there among our Irish and Anglo-=Irish friends and acquaintances. The cost of living furnished a lively topic for public persiflage and private ruefulness. And finally, by infinite gradations, the submarine menace began to define itself in our minds.

Now and again as the winter wore on big steamships would slip quietly into port and anchor in the road-stead or make fast to the Deep Water Quay. Sometimes they would show oddly-shaped packages, tarpaulin-covered, on their decks; and when later on the vessels vanished over night we were allowed to suspect that special pains had been taken to keep the U-boats—in which we still hardly believed—from intercepting them. It was on one of these steamships, which chanced to carry some two-score Americans, that we made the acquaintance of Captain William Thomas Turner, who three months later was in command of the Cunard steamer *Lusitania*.

The first actual evidence of the presence of submarines off Queenstown, as nearly as I can recall, related to the *Anglo-Californian*. Walking into town one dismal winter morning along the Deep Water Quay I found there a big freighter with a curiously battered funnel and superstructures; and noticed Constabulary officers carrying a burlap gunnysack down the gang-plank. The sack contained the dismembered fragments of the late Master of the *Anglo-Californian*; and it was followed by the mutilated corpses of eight of his staunch seamen. Alfred Noyes, in his "Open Boats," gives the wireless dialogue between the *Anglo-Californian* and the naval vessels coming to her assistance during her three-hour flight from the submarine; but Mr. Noyes does not mention that when the master was blown to pieces on his bridge his son stepped forward instantly and took the wheel, ultimately bringing the ship safe into Queenstown.

Only one other submarine incident transpired during that winter,—the case of the *Wayfarer*. Like the escape of the *Anglo-Californian*, the saving of the *Wayfarer* after she had been torpedoed showed that the original German submarines were by no means as efficient as the later ones have since become. Or it may be that the incident showed merely the exceptional solidity of the ship's bulkheads. At any rate we understood that five out of the eleven compartments of the *Wayfarer* filled with water as a result of the submarine attack; and that the remaining six compartments kept the ship afloat during the one-hundred-and-fifty-mile tow into Queenstown!

Except for these comparatively unimportant cases, the *Lusitania* catastrophe came upon Queenstown without forewarnings. I sometimes think of the entire submarine campaign as similar to some vile and gigantic reptile which has made its appearance head foremost, and whose loathe-some body is still dragging itself past. The *Lusitania* horror was the hissing head of the reptile.

The fact and terms of the German warning to Americans against taking passage on Allied steamships were duly cabled to the United Kingdom; and we read in the Cork newspapers Count von Bernstorff's cool statement that, "Travelers sailing in the war zone on ships of Great Britain and her Allies do so at their own risk." The reference to the *Lusitania* was obvious enough; but personally it never entered my mind for a moment that the Germans would actually perpetrate an attack upon her. The culpability of such an act seemed too blatant and raw for an intelligent people to take upon themselves. We had not realized yet the German deficiency in human comprehensions, a deficiency based, I believe, upon the destruction by German economic and governmental conditions of the German sense of humor. (One often hears expressions of wonder as to how a people so sentimental as the Germans can be at the same time so cruel. My own suggestion is that both sentimentality and cruelty arise from absence of humor.) Then, in addition, I did not believe that the submarines had yet shown any striking power equal to the task of attacking and destroying a ship as huge, well built and fast as the *Lusitania*. I was not alone in my attitude; for there was among the general public in Queenstown, at least in the educated classes, no apparent expectation that the threat was anything more than bluster.

Accordingly the afternoon of May 7, 1915, found me engaged in a painstaking revision-transcription of a long annual commercial report upon the condition of Counties Cork, Kerry, Tipperary, Waterford, Clare and Limerick. My Vice-Consul, however,

Mr. Lewis C. Thompson, of Norfolk, Virginia, had formed a more correct impression of the probabilities; and spent a good part of the day in various offices along the waterfront where news might be expected to develop. At two-thirty in the afternoon he came hurriedly up the stairs—the American Consulate at Queenstown is on a second floor above a bar-room—saying that there was a wildfire rumor about town that the *Lusitania* had been attacked. Stepping quickly to the windows, we could see a very unusual stir in the harbor; and as we looked the harbor's "mosquito fleet" of tugs, tenders and trawlers, some two dozen in all, began to steam past the town toward the harbor-mouth.

I immediately went to the telephone and called up Paymaster Norcocks, the secretary to Rear-Admiral Sir Charles Coke, and said rather apologetically,

"I hear there is some sort of street rumor that the *Lusitania* has been attacked." I could hardly believe my ears when the response came, "It's true, Mr. Frost. We fear she is gone." The stress on the word "true" gave me an unforgettable mental shock; and I listened rather mechanically to the meager information the Paymaster could give me-the wireless message of distress, "Come at once. Big list to starboard. Ten miles off Kinsale," and the telephone confirmation by watchers on the shore at the Old Head of Kinsale that the *Lusitania* had disappeared.

I must have spent ten or fifteen minutes pacing the floor of the office, adjusting my mind to the fact of the disaster, and turning over the possible ways in which the Consulate could be of service. Even then, I am frank to say, no very definite chain of action came into my mind; and as a matter of fact throughout the days and weeks that followed our course was dictated almost from moment to moment by the circumstances that clamored about us for attention.

My first act was to telegraph briefly to Consul-General Skinner and Ambassador Page at London, giving the astounding facts. Then I went down to the Munster&Leinster Bank and procured a supply of British specie for loans.

We all conjectured that a good share of the survivors would land at Kinsale, a town of nearly three thousand people, which was only nine or ten miles from the scene of the sinking, while Queenstown was twenty-three or twenty-four miles. After serious hesitation as to whether I ought not personally to proceed to Kinsale, I decided to send Mr. Thompson. He took one hundred pounds and went up to Cork to hire an automobile, reaching Kinsale about seven o'clock. I had simply instructed him to do anything and everything possible for the comfort of the survivors, and to call on the Consulate freely for money or assistance. It developed, however, that only nine of the survivors actually landed at Kinsale; and Mr. Thompson very energetically induced his chauffeur to drive back to Cork in the darkness, so that before ten o'clock in the evening he was with us on the Cunard Wharf.

Offers of assistance from local people of American affiliations began to come in between four and five o'clock. Mrs. John Dinan, of Knockevin, not only offered to shelter survivors but had the splendid good-sense to send us at once a big hamper of warm and comfortable clothing. Mrs. Richard Townsend, Mrs. Benjamin Haughton, and Mrs. William Leahy were generous in their offers, and later on proved to be untiring in their efforts among the American lady survivors. Mrs. Frost came early to the Consulate, and during the evening twice made trips to our home with survivors.

Consul William L. Jenkins, who happened fortunately to be detailed as assistant at the Dublin Consulate, called up by long distance telephone to offer his services; and made his appearance next morning after an awkward night trip. Mr. John Dinan, Jr., American Consular Agent at Limerick, left his large business interests there and came down to Queenstown for Saturday and Sunday; and his brother, my friend the late Lieutenant George W. Dinan, then a student at Cork University, worked in the Consulate for several days with great sympathy and intelligence.

At about six o'clock it occurred to me that possibly Mr. Page and Mr. Skinner at London might not have relayed my telegraphic report to Washington, or that the Department of State might appreciate direct reports; and I accordingly cabled to the Secretary of State. From that time forward, to obviate delays, I reported by cable straight to Washington, sending the same messages, of course, by telegraph to my superiors at London. The practice thus begun continued for over two years, and ran into several thousand dollars in cost. Washington certainly kept its finger on the pulse of the submarine campaign without any intermission, whether German promises were present or absent.

The fact that no news could be procured from the disaster until the rescue ships arrived, since these ships were all too small to carry wireless, gave a few hours' respite for completing arrangements for the reception of the victims. The heaviest burden fell upon the Cunard Company's agent, Mr. J.J. Murphy, and his assistants, and they wrought miracles in organizing the hotels and lodging-houses and clothing-stores. The British naval and military authorities provided hospital accommodation, stretcher-bearers, and no little private hospitality. The Constabulary and the Queenstown civil authorities made morgue and hospital arrangements. The local volunteer first-aid corps were mustered; and among the numerous medical men who gave devoted service throughout the days following may be mentioned the late Major Crofts, R.A.M.C., the universally beloved head of the Military Hospital, and Doctor Ralph Hodges, Doctor Richard Townsend, and Doctor William O'Connor, all of Queenstown. To my mind the most valuable single preparatory act of initiative was Captain Wallace Dickie's summons of the volunteer motor ambulance corps of Cork. Some forty or fifty automobiles came down from Cork as a result, under Mr. Winder, a leading Cork attorney, and rendered excellent service in distributing the wounded and exhausted victims.

At this point perhaps it may be permissible to take up some of the facts regarding the actual disaster itself, even though our information is not firsthand. The Consulate talked fully and freely with scores of survivors while their impressions were still very fresh; and we procured written narrative statements from most of the intelligent American survivors. Naturally, too, we took an interest in going carefully over the extensive testimony taken by Lord Mersey's commission of inquiry. Thus altogether perhaps as good an idea of what transpired has been gathered as any formed by the persons who passed through the disaster but had neither occasion nor opportunity to gain a general perspective view of it.

CHAPTER III

THE CATASTROPHE PROPER

THE WEATHER CONDITIONS ON THAT FATEFUL FRIDAY AFTERNOON were exceptionally lovely. The wonderful South Irish littoral was bathed in clear spring sunshine, and the sea was as smooth as a mirror. The ship was traveling comfortably at the rate of from sixteen to eighteen knots per hour, a speed dictated by the hours of the tides at the dangerous Liverpool bar. The ship's boats had been swung out, and a life-belt drill had been held on the previous evening. It was necessary for Captain Turner to approach the coast long enough to take a formal landfall, because it would have been hazardous to run clear into the Liverpool bar on dead reckoning only; but the Captain delayed this operation until the most advantageous time of day and until he was within ready reach of help from Queenstown.

Most of the passengers, including as fine an aggregation of representative Americans as the "Lucy" ever carried, had finished their luncheons and were dispersed about the decks enjoying the sunshine and admiring the tender emerald-green of the Irish coastline-the Old Head of Kinsale being eight miles off the port beam. Suddenly, at eight minutes past two o'clock (Greenwich Mean Time), a torpedo was seen leaping swiftly through the surface from the seaward-"cutting the water like a razor"-and some of the passengers even discerned the conning tower of a submarine about three hundred yards off the starboard bow. The torpedo struck between the third and fourth funnels, and by its exploding crash converted that splendid scene into the most hideous and criminal catastrophe that human history has known.

Within thirty seconds of the impact a second explosion took place; presumably an engine-room explosion, since the engines were immediately put out of control and the lights went out all through the interior of the ship. The testimony as to a second torpedo is confusing; but in view of the prior announcements and subsequent conduct of the Germans a second torpedo would not strengthen our certainty that they had determined to destroy the ship regardless of consequences.

Captain Turner immediately ordered the wheel hard a-starboard to turn the ship to port toward the land; and a little later, to facilitate the taking to the lifeboats, sought to have the engines reversed to take the way off the ship. The engines failed to respond. The wireless operator got away the message to the Admiralty already quoted.

On account of the speed at which the ship's momentum was still carrying her forward, Captain Turner judged it best not to attempt for the time being to launch the lifeboats. He had every reason for believing that his fine ship would remain afloat much longer than she did. A little later, when the speed was flagging, he ordered the starboard boats to be lowered; but the confusion had by that time become great.

Confidence in the *Lusitania's* floating capacity was based upon her special construction. In most steamers, as the reader knows, a series of cross-walls divide the ship into cross-sections, so that if the hull is pierced the water can flood into only one or two sections. In the *Lusitania*, in order to make this protection still more positive, there were not only these "transverse bulkheads" but also "longitudinal bulkheads," or walls running lengthwise through the ship along the coal bunkers. Thus the water, upon entering, was not only confined to certain cross-sections but also to a single side of these sections. This arrangement has been known as "battleship construction," because the idea originated with Navy designers. It results in increasing the buoyancy of the stricken ship but also in increasing the sharpness or steepness of any list or cant which she may assume. In the case of the *Lusitania* this extreme list-which at one time was not less than forty degrees-seems to have been fatal, because it is believed to have brought certain apertures in the ship's side beneath the waterline. But any board of experienced nautical men or marine architects would have believed precisely as Captain Turner did that the *Lusitania*, wounded as she was, would remain afloat far longer than eighteen minutes. The *Titanic* experience is really irrelevant.

To the eternal credit of humanity stands the absence of panic and terror when the *Lusitania* was foundering. Mr. Frohman's noble remark that "Death is the most fascinating adventure in life"; Mr. Vanderbilt's efforts in saving women and children; and Staff-Captain Anderson's self-immolation in getting away the starboard lifeboats—all are perfectly typical of the air of calm energy which prevailed. The contradictory evidence on this point is negligible. The overwhelming testimony is that the catastrophe was a large-scale proof of the innate courage of the human heart.

But of confusion, of chaos, of disorder, there were inevitably superabundant evidences. Unskilled persons in attempting to handle the falls or pulleys which lowered the lifeboats made awful failures; and several boats were released at one end only, spilling their occupants out into the sea. Other boats were never freed from the davits at all, and were therefore dragged down with their occupants when the ship sank. Still other boats were broken by lurching inboard or against the side of the vessel. For example, the second port boat swung in against the deck-wall of the smoking-room, and crushed to death or hopelessly crippled some thirty or forty passengers who were huddled together waiting for its preparation. In none of these accidents can strong blame be imputed to the persons on board the *Lusitania*. Probably instances did occur in which better judgment might have saved lives; but on the whole the standard of conduct not only as to courage but as to self-possession and resourcefulness was amazingly high.

The most heart-piercing scenes were enacted. Husbands beheld their wives crushed and flung hurtling like debris. Gentle elderly ladies such as Mrs. Elbert Hubbard met death with quiet an-d pathetic dignity; and I want to insist that they did not merely die, but were killed. The multiplication of murder does not make it any the less murder; and if a personal enemy of yours should deliberately ride down in a motor car your gray-haired mother and dash her brains out on the pavement his crime would be identical with that perpetrated against the gentlewomen on the *Lusitania*.

Men with broken limbs calmly strove in the water to preserve not only their own lives but the lives of others. Little children drowned in speechless terror while looking into the very eyes of their powerless mothers. Many of these people were our fellow-countrymen; and the fact that they do not happen to have been relatives or friends is purely fortuitous.

The vessel steadied herself onto a fairly even keel about ten minutes after the torpedo explosion, presumably because the water broke its way across into the port side. But before sinking she gradually resumed her list to starboard, and in disappearing she lurched heavily in this direction. More than one-half, probably, of her occupants were at this time—twenty-six minutes past two o'clock—still on her decks or seated in unlaunched lifeboats; although perhaps this estimate should include part of the numerous persons who were swimming in the water in the lee of the stagnating hull. At all events a large number of men and women were hurled into the water by the lurch which just preceded the foundering, or flung themselves into the sea just previously to it; and they were followed by a shower of spars, chairs, and various deck-litter which stunned and killed many of them.

The *Lusitania* sank bow foremost; and her propellers were even at one time slightly above the water, since some of the lifeboats took hold of them in pushing off. At the last, the weight of evidence shows, the stern projected at an abrupt angle. One survivor told me very vividly of standing high on the stern after the bow had partly disappeared and gazing down sixty feet or more upon the impotent swarms of human creatures twisting crazily like flies underneath and upon the surface of the clear green sea. It seems probable that the prow touched the sea-floor before the stern sank. The depth of the sea was only sixty fathoms, or three hundred and sixty feet, at the spot of the foundering; and this is just one-half the length of the ship. The feebleness of the suction in the vortex surprised many witnesses.

The reverse force after the vortex, on the other hand—a sort of regurgitation by the ocean of human bodies and debris—astonished the survivors by its violence. Interior explosions seem to have taken place in the ship as she sank; and they not only killed many people directly but probably also accounted for the great eruptive force with which swimmers, corpses, deck-chairs, oars, and a large mass of wreckage were shot churning upwards to the surface. The danger of being crushed or injured during this phase of the disaster was much greater than during the suction phase which had preceded it. A swimmer looking back describes the spot as "a mound of water," foaming above the general level of the sea for an appreciable space of time. A curious minor-keyed sound of horror issued from and sprang along the water, almost as though the sea itself, they said, were moaning in conscious revulsion. It was of course merely the blending of human cries of fright and pain, in which the treble of women's voices was a constituent.

The rotary twist taken in the final plunge caused the huge funnels and the wireless antenna to bear down upon and mutilate and kill large numbers of people in the water. My friend, Mr. Frederick J. Gauntlett, told me of being caught in the back by a descending aerial and being carried forty feet below the surface before he could turn himself around to get his hands on the wire and free himself. Captain Turner, who was determined, despite his sixty-two years of age, to go down on his bridge like a true British master-mariner, is said to have calculated his danger from the wireless aerials with the greatest coolness. As the water closed about him he felt his way up along the mast by means of the flag-halyards, and when he judged himself near the network of wires he kicked strongly out from the mast and was able to come free of them to the surface. Young Mr. Adams, of Chicago, describes how a collapsible boat which he was just planning to get into commission was cut in two like so much paper by the sweep of a descending wire.

There is quite a little testimony to the effect that the German submarine emerged for a brief interval at this juncture, to survey the scene, submerging again rather promptly; but the fact cannot be regarded as well established, and—newspaper paragraphs to the contrary—I have never alluded to this circumstance in discussing the disaster either publicly or privately.

Most of the lifeboats which remained afloat, some sixteen in all, counting the collapsible boats, now returned over the scene of the foundering; although one or two of them which could have taken in more survivors made off rather discreditably toward the land. Dozens of men performed prodigies in utilizing the collapsible boats and rescuing their less fortunate fellow-passengers. Lord

Mersey singles out an eighteen-year-old British sailor boy, Leslie N. Morton, whose pluck and vigor saved many lives; and there were of course many other persons whose conduct cannot but excite unstinted admiration. If I were asked to furnish an honor-roll of American survivors who behaved with special heroism I should name Mrs. Theodore Naish, William McMullen Adams (aet. nineteen years), James H. Brooks, Frederick J. Gauntlett, Charles E. Lauriat, Jr., and Isaac Lehmann; and doubtless a fuller knowledge of the facts might expand this list considerably.

The collapsible lifeboats had for the most part been unfastened from their places by the ship's seamen during the brief moments before the sinking; and this type of boats must have accounted for at least one-third of all the life-saving. There were exciting scenes as efforts were made to get them properly opened and mounted in the water while swarms of exhausted swimmers were crowding about them and onto them. It is hard for a timid person, unaccustomed to remaining in the water, to realize the necessity and practicability of waiting while adjustments are being made; but nevertheless calmness and courage were the general rule. In a striking number of instances the disaster resulted in the survival of the physically fittest; but these persons did not save themselves at the expense of others. On the contrary their self-preservation was usually or often incidental to their efforts to save others.

The scenes among the debris cast up from the wreck were so excruciating as to defy description. Drowned bodies of women and children were numerous, and many had been mangled or disfigured in the surge and grinding of the wreckage so as to stain the ocean with blood. A British survivor heavily bandaged from an operation performed in America told me of clinging to a waterlogged boat and watching the drowning struggles of a group composed of a woman and infant and a gray-bearded, feeble old man. Overcrowded lifeboats passed friends or relatives of their occupants and helplessly saw these dear ones slip beneath the surface from prostration or injuries. Some corpses bore life-preservers improperly fastened, so that they floated with only the lower part of the body exposed.

A British lady was sucked down a smokestack, and then when the water met the fires was expelled by the steam with great violence. Much of her clothing was torn from her person, and she was so begrimed with soot and cinders that her own husband did not recognize her an hour or so later when she hailed him from a neighboring boat. An American business man, fighting his way through the wreckage to the surface, felt himself wrapped and snared by ropes, as he supposed, but used his arms to raise himself to the air. Once on the surface it developed that the supposed ropes were the clinging arms of three different people. The entire group was saved.

Elbert Hubbard, according to a very responsible American friend, found himself alone in the water after the *Lusitania* had sunk, and swam to a cylindrical steel drum broken out from the corner of a life-raft. The water, although not frigid, was sharply chilly; and as he felt himself growing numb he made a stout struggle to climb up onto the cylinder. By the time he had been able to throw his weight across it, the cylinder revolved slowly in the water, and plunged him off on the other side. He tried this a second time and a third time, with the same result of being thrown off by the rotating of the cylinder under his weight. By this time the shock and exposure and struggle had proved too much for our genial veteran philosopher; his strength failed him, his hands slipped from the drum, and he sank half-conscious to his death. The lifeboat from which this incident was witnessed was preoccupied with its own difficulties and with other rescue work at the time; but somehow I fancy that the big-hearted Fra would hardly have chosen to die otherwise than as he did, much as he would deplore the interruption of his life-work at a time when it was never of greater service to his country.

A lifeboat rowing about had its attention caught by an intermittent flashing light on an undulation of the sea several rods away, and proceeded to the spot largely out of curiosity. It found a circular lifebuoy clasped by the hand of a drowned lady whose body depended entirely beneath the surface. But on one of the two or three unsubmerged fingers a great diamond was flashing in the sunlight. The possession of this valuable bauble saved from an unknown ocean resting-place the remains of a distinguished American lady chemist, who was journeying to England to meet King George and other eminent people.

Before resuming the thread of events at the arrival of the rescue ships from Queenstown, it may be well to summarize the loss of life and property resulting from the disaster. The property loss was of course severe. The reader perhaps recalls that the *Lusitania* was one-seventh of a mile—seven hundred and sixty-nine feet-in length; and had a width of eighty—eight feet, a depth of sixty feet, a displacement of 41,400 tons, and an indicated horse-power of sixty-eight thousand. The combined value of the huge ship and her cargo on this last voyage, the Cunard Company tell me, was nearly eleven million dollars. It is doubtful if any of the most pretentious hotels in the United States would constitute, if destroyed today by a sudden earthquake, a property loss equal to the *Lusitania' s.*

One may go further and say that probably the loss of life, if the New Willard Hotel at Washington were to be engulfed in the earth, would be less important both quantitatively and qualitatively than was the loss of life from the *Lusitania.* The ship's passenger list was 1,265 persons, and the crew numbered 694 persons, so that the ship carried just short of two thousand souls—1,959 to be precise. Of this two thousand practically twelve hundred—1,195—persons perished. The dead comprised, in round numbers, eight hundred men, three hundred women, and one hundred children; and of the children, thirty-five were infants in arms. It should be emphasized that the percentage of the crew saved was virtually the same as the percentage of the passengers—viz., 42 percent of the crew and 37.5 percent of the passengers—and this in spite of the fact that the crew were all able-bodied males while the passengers were more than two-fifths women and children. Certainly the crew did nobly toward saving passengers.

Coming to the figures for American citizens, we find that out of 189 Americans on board the Lusitania 123 were killed or drowned, and only 66 survived to tread solid earth again. The American death-roster included, among others, Elbert Hubbard, Charles Frohman, Charles Klein, and Justus Miles Forman, as men of letters or arts; Alfred G. Vanderbilt, Harry J. Keser, A.C. Bilicke, William S. Hodges, Albert L. Hopkins, and—greatest of all who died in the disaster—Dr. J.S. Pearson, as business men; and Lindon W. Bates, Herbert S. Stone, Mrs. R.D. Shymer, and Captain James Blaine Miller, as persons distinguished in various ways. Most of these persons are too well known to warrant any comment; but possibly some of them were not so familiar to the general American public as they might well have been.

Lindon W. Bates was the first assistant and right-hand man of Mr. Hoover in the Belgian Relief Commission work. His clear-headed efficiency and energy would have been literally beyond money value to the United States at the present time if he had been spared to remain at Mr. Hoover's side. A.C. Bilicke was one of the wealthiest and most public-spirited citizens of Los Angeles, and had been a leader in many forward-looking enterprises, both industrial and humanitarian, on the Pacific Coast. Herbert S. Stone, son of Melville Stone of the Associated Press, was a man of marked gifts and physical and mental vitality, already on the road to a substantial independent reputation. Captain J.B. Miller, of the United States Coast and Geodetic Survey — "Zeke" Miller we used to call him when he was a football hero at Oberlin — was one of the most useful and promising officers in the Survey.

I have, of course, expressed my own personal opinion in referring to Dr. J.S. Pearson as the greatest man who perished from the *Lusitania*. This eminent American business man was president of the Newport News Drydock and Shipbuilding Company, and had carried through large electric-power undertakings in Mexico, the Argentine, and finally in old Spain. He represented in its perfection, I believe, the finest type produced by our nation at its present stage of development, the type of the constructive idealist, the business pioneer and industrial creative genius. And his abilities would unquestionably have contributed greatly to meeting the present crisis in American tonnage-construction had he not perished.

CHAPTER IV

RESCUE AND RELIEF WORK

THE RESCUE CRAFT FROM QUEENSTOWN BEGAN TO REACH THE SCAT-
tered lifeboats and flotsam from the *Lusitania* between five and
six o'clock. Some of the lifeboats had reached fishing-boats a few
miles off Kinsale before the tugs arrived, and their passengers had
to be retransferred to the latter. The steamship *Katarina*, flying
the Greek flag, had also appeared on the scene and picked up the
occupants of two or three lifeboats, which she turned over to the
rescue fleet. Several times the Queenstown boats were met with
the hail, "We're all right. Go on to the others!"

Probably no person, who was still alive at the time the help
arrived, was left in the water to die, as several of the tugs and
tenders beat back and forth across the sea for two or three hours.
Of course the coma which follows numbing in the chilly water
resembles death very closely. During the hours preceding rescue
quite a few apparently drowned persons were taken into the lifeboats and resuscitated; and there were some startling cases of this
on board the tugs en route to Queenstown. I saw one handsome
young woman at Queenstown who had been dragged out from a
pile of corpses on a rescue ship because of a flutter of the eyelids.
She seemed none the worse for her experience. On the other

hand, two or three survivors passed away between the time they were rescued and the arrival at Queenstown.

The rough and cordial kindness shown by the seamen of the rescue fleet was much commented upon by the survivors. These craft had gone out so hastily that they were not equipped with many relief appliances; but they were able to supply shelter, heat, rude clothing, and warm drink to a majority of the survivors who needed them; and the crews vied with one another in giving spontaneously their garments, food and even money to the unfortunates whom they were saving. The impulses toward pity and helpfulness which the disaster universally inspired in Ireland found their first, and very fitting, outward manifestation or expression in the acts of the men of the Queenstown harbor fleet.

We saw the ghastly procession of these rescue ships as they landed the living and the dead that night under the flaring gas torches along the Queenstown water-front. The arrivals began soon after eight o'clock and continued at close intervals until about eleven o'clock. Ship after ship would come up out of the darkness, and sometimes two or three could be just descried awaiting their turns in the cloudy night, to discharge bruised and shuddering women, crippled and half-clothed men, and a few wide-eyed little children whose minds were still revolving blankly this new experience of human existence of God's footstool. Women caught at our sleeves and begged desperately for word of their husbands; and men with choking efforts at matter-of-factness moved ceaselessly from group to group, seeking a lost daughter or sister or even bride. Piles of corpses like cordwood began to appear among the paint-kegs and coils of rope on the shadowy old wharves. Ever;y: voice in that great mixed assemblage was pitched in unconscious undertones, broken now and then b painful coughing-fits or suppressed hysteria.

The intention was to have all the boats land at the Cunard Wharf and the wharf next to it; but as the process of discharging wounded or prostrated survivors was sometimes rather lengthy and toilsome, two or three of the boats, upon their own initiative, landed at neighboring wharves where no arrangements had been made to meet them. In all the cases, however, some member of the Consulate's staff managed to hail the boats as they drew in, and to get from their commanders or from some responsible persons an estimate of the number of survivors and corpses on board. Thus shortly after eleven o'clock we cabled to the Department of State provisional total estimates which stood for a day or two as the only ones available. The Cunard Company was unwilling to give out any estimate until they could be sure that it was approximately correct.

We first requested the various registrars to procure the nationality of each registrant, and then at intervals, as time could be found amid the welfare work, we made the rounds of the desks and copied off the names of the Americans as they appeared. The lists thus built up were cabled from time to time to Washington, and although the orthography was often defective—and sometimes the nationality incorrect—the margin of error was not so great as we feared at the time. Several American survivors volunteered their aid in our tasks, and proved devoted and useful from the moment they stepped onto the wharves. Through these and through such officials as could give the matter attention we passed the word around that all Americans should report at the Consulate on the following—Saturday—morning.

There were two or three Americans, I regret to say, and a number of persons of other nationalities, who landed without injury or exhaustion and straightway proceeded to the best hotel at Cork and thence on their way to London without so much as a backward glance or a thought of pity for their companions in the tragedy.

There was little immediate physical assistance which the Consulate could extend. Lodging and food and clothing were amply provided by the Cunard Company, and the Naval and Military authorities. Scores of the private residents of Queenstown took survivors into their ho es utterly irrespective of nationality. Many Americans were guests in British and Irish houses, and in the same way it happened that the American colony—if that word can be applied to so small a group of people—entertained a number of British subjects.

It is doubtless true that the quarters supplied at some of the lodging-houses were not quite what we were anxious to provide; but there is a limit to what a town of ten thousand people, nearly all working-people, can provide in this direction upon less than six hours' notice. It was observable, also, that such complaints as reached our ears were mainly from survivors from those rescue ships which landed at wharves they had been asked to avoid.

The distribution of survivors for the night proceeded with much expedition. Considerably before midnight the Cunard officers were almost empty of the agitated and pitiable refugees who had overflowed them two hours earlier. The blanket-wrapped or underwear-clad figures, the rolling eyes of the excitable foreign survivors, the bandages and slings, and the hoarse voices and hacking coughs of sufferers from exposure—all these elements of the weird and unforgettable scene vanished away in an incredibly brief space of time, it seemed to us.

Between midnight and morning the principal official activities consisted in having the corpses—of which some 160 were brought ashore with the survivors—laid out in the three improvised morgues, and in arranging transportation for the living on the following day.

At about two o'clock in the morning we turned our attention to ascertaining the facts as to how the disaster took place — hour of the day, absence of warning, speed, weather, measures toward safety, and the like. Very few capable witnesses could be found still awake and available; but by four o'clock we had managed to cable a resume sufficiently full for general provisional purposes.

By five o'clock I was in bed and asleep; and I did not reach the Consulate again until eight-thirty Saturday morning. I have seen frequent statements to the effect that I got no sleep for several days after the *Lusitania* disaster; but although this was the case in one or two subsequent disasters, it does not happen to be true as to the *Lusitania*. It is a fact that we saw daylight lighten the sky for several mornings, and even during June we were still working until midnight; but we always took pains to get the maximum possible amount of rest, as any sensible men would have done in the same circumstances. The consular work entailed by the *Lusitania* tragedy reached its peak some six weeks after the event; and probably was occupying a full half of our time at the end of the year in December. Our bound correspondence in the case constitutes about twelve inches of solid reading-matter, and any person familiar with office work will realize what that means.

During Saturday our primary attention was to the instant needs of the American survivors. The great majority of the Americans reported at the Consulate in the course of the day.

The first effort of the Cunard and Naval officials was naturally to forward the able-bodied survivors to their homes, or English destinations, at the earliest possible moment; and the majority of the victims left Queenstown by the afternoon or evening trains on Saturday. The Great Southern&Western Railway officials with great foresight took the full names and addresses of each survivor to whom transportation was issued; and these lists were useful later in checking up and amplifying our own.

One feature of the work at the Consulate on Saturday consisted in the loaning of small sums of money to Americans who needed it temporarily; and our inquiries as to the need were not too searching. We took the addresses, and the personal promissory notes, of the persons involved, and disposed of about one hundred and forty pounds sterling. I think about one hundred pounds of this was eventually returned. Some of the poorer survivors took the attitude that their injuries entitled them to reparation from the Government, and evidently thought it just not to return the money they had borrowed. The loans were a great convenience to all concerned; and Ambassador Page and the Department of State very promptly and fully backed up the Consulate in all such special disbursements, not only as to loans but as to attention to American corpses and advertisements and rewards concerning the salving of bodies. Whenever possible we of course extended relief in the form of clothing or of minor personal attentions in cases of illness or wounds.

The Consulate had been immediately instructed by Mr. Bryan, then Secretary of State, to procure more or less formal statements from the American survivors, in order that the circumstances of the crime might promptly rest upon written evidence. Accordingly the preparation of statements was one of the matters which we had to urge upon the survivors even from the first. At the outset the narratives procured were rather brief and elliptical; but in the course of two or three days some fifteen or twenty quite full and reliable American statements were secured, and eventually this number was almost doubled. The facts as to the disaster, in my judgment, can be drawn from this material quite adequately and satisfactorily; and if ever published it will form a companion-piece to the report of the Mersey Commission of Inquiry.

The work of assisting survivors m ascertaining whether their relatives or companions on the lost vessel had been saved was the most distressing of our duties. We were quickly overwhelmed with inquiries about missing relatives, not only from Americans but from persons of British and other nationalities. Widows, widowers, parents, orphans, brothers and friends of deceased victims crowded the Consulate steadily for three or four days; and in some cases appeared daily for weeks after the tragedy. When the relatives and friends from London and the continent reached Queenstown, and the cabled inquiries from America began to accumulate, the number of specific inquiries upon the Consulate, with descriptions of the missing persons, mounted up into the hundreds. The personal visits from bereaved people were often poignant to the last degree, especially when such visits came to be repeated time after time, at intervals of hours or days, with increasing hopelessness and grief as the absence of news became tantamount to certainty of death.

Without mentioning the names of these stricken Americans, to spread their private sorrows out for public inspection, I must mention two or three of the cases which will always stand out in my memory. An American business man who had in middle life been married to a beautiful and comparatively young wife came over from London to learn her fate and that of the two sturdy little sons whom she was bringing over to him. Not a particle of information was ever forthcoming even as to their having been seen after the ship was struck, to say nothing of their deaths or the recovery of their bodies; and the tragic spectacle of that father and husband, whose entire life had been wrapped up in his family, haunted the Consulate for a fortnight. Another case was that of an American father and mother who had lost two beautiful little daughters, and who were notably devoted in their efforts at least to have the bodies recovered. Nothing could be accomplished, however, and their hopeless depression was pitiable.

An incident which illustrates the agonizing quality of the days through which Queenstown was living is that of the Blank families. Two married couples by the same name were among the saloon passengers of the *Lusitania*, and by a caprice of fate in one case the husband and in the other the wife was saved. At different houses in Queenstown these mismated survivors were for quite a time buoyed up in their recuperation by the assurance that their wife or husband respectively had been saved. Only after a day or more, I was told, were they brought together to confront one another in a sickening realization that in each case their nearest and dearest had been taken instead of spared.

One widow whose husband had been an admirable and charming American man of affairs seemed to be completely unnerved by her loss. Her sorrow reminded me of that of a child, so utter and blind did it seem. Her mind, her friends state, has never quite recovered from the shock; and her character has altered permanently. Another American widow whose loss was equally severe was fortified by an earnest and consecrated piety, which made her constancy of grief perhaps even harder to witness, so rapt was her spirit. I cannot imagine a more complete exemplification of the consolations which religion affords to its votaries.

A fine anodyne against sorrow was the volunteer personal relief work carried on by some whose personal losses had been cruel. A stalwart young American university man, for example, who had lost an elder brother, plunged heart and soul into the work of having the utmost possible number of bodies recovered, partly in the hope of finding his brother's corpse, and his cooperation with the Consulate in scattering reward posters and keeping in touch with the fisher-people and other lifesaving agencies along the Cork and Kerry coasts by means of a motorcycle was a positive godsend to us.

Another survivor, who, however, lost only friends on the *Lusitania*, proved indefatigable in conducting relief work. He appeared to consider that his own preservation imposed upon him a debt to his fellow-beings; and expended time, energy, sympathy and money around Queenstown with the utmost freedom for ten days after the disaster. At the time the ship was sunk he had been suffering from a severe cold, and moreover during the three hours which he spent in the water his legs had been badly scraped by wreckage; but he limped indomitably about the town, except for two days in bed when his legs became inflamed, and in several matters was very helpful to the Consulate.

CHAPTER V

DEALING WITH THE DEAD

THE AMERICAN NEWSPAPER CORRESPONDENTS ARRIVED IN
Queenstown from London on Saturday noon, and we were very
glad to have them promptly make the Consulate their rendezvous.
After my three years of absence from America it was pleasant to
come into contact again with a group of keen and well-grained
Americans; and it is my impression that the "stories" cabled to
most of the metropolitan newspapers in America must have
been quite sane and dependable. Norman Hapgood came over
to Queenstown to prosecute inquiries for the body of his friend,
Justus Miles Forman, but I think made no direct journalistic use
of his visit.

One or two of the reporters for the semi-sensational type of
American journals were perhaps a little over-eager to pick up
"human interest stuff," and telegraphed verbal pictures of discon-
solateness and neediness which gave incorrect impressions. The
story about the pathetic neglect of the body of Charles Frohman
belongs in this category; and this brings me back to our tasks in
connection with the American corpses.

By Saturday afternoon I began to have opportunity to divert a
few minutes' attention from the living to the dead. Vice Consul

Thompson had by that time secured a fairly accurate list of identified American bodies, and we began telegraphing for instructions
from relatives as to the disposition of these, especially whether
it was desired that they be embalmed and shipped home or be
buried at Queenstown, or be shipped in leaden caskets without
embalming. The cabling process seemed to be discouragingly
slow as to results, although the Department of State aided greatly.

There were a number of bodies of important Americans
which we saw at once ought indisputably to be embalmed and returned to the United States; and at different times during Saturday
afternoon and evening I must have spent a couple of hours tele-
phoning to various medical and undertaking offices. The process
of preserving dead bodies seems to be relatively unnecessary in
the United Kingdom, owing to the coolness of the climate and the
shortness of the distances over which corpses have to be shipped
in the small territory of the British Isles.

By Saturday midnight, therefore, which was within a few
hours of the time when we could decently turn our attention to
the problem, Mr. Frohman's body was provided for. On Sunday
our surgeon came down from Cork with materials and assistants,
and set up an improvised operating room to the rear of the Cunard
offices, and for five days he or his assistants were constantly occupied. Twice I visited this work-room on business errands, and
I shall never forget the sight I saw the second time—the body on
the embalmer's slab of a beautiful American girl who was scarcely
ten days a bride at the time of her murder by the Germans. She lay
like a statue typifying assassinated innocence.

On Sunday we continued to make the Consulate, as far as possible, a medium of exchange for information between the survivors, relatives of victims, steamship offices, press and Government.
On Sunday noon Captain A. Miller and Captain W.A. Castle,

U.S.A., then special military attaches to the American Ambassador at London, reached Queenstown on his behalf; and their active sympathy and helpfulness among all classes of survivors formed an unfailing source for gratitude on the part of every American during the next four days. On Sunday afternoon we went, with Consul Jenkins, to pay official respects to Admiral Coke; and that interview was extremely interesting.

We had now formulated the policy that all identified first-cabin American dead should be embalmed, deeming it better to err on the safe side; and that all other identified American bodies should be sealed into leaden caskets so that they could be returned to America whenever desired. This policy Captains Castle and Miller indorsed on behalf of the Embassy, thus sharing the financial responsibility.

Mr. Thompson had meanwhile been wrestling with the problem of procuring suitable caskets. All the good caskets in stock at Cork and Queenstown were instantly absorbed by the demand; and we found that for a good share of the bodies leaden cases must be specially constructed at Cork—a process quicker and less expensive than sending to London.

It ought to be stated that in general the American relatives on behalf of whom these steps were taken proved to be more than ready to repay the expenditures, unduly large as the latter must have seemed to them. In a very few cases of mistaken nationality, or where religion made the embalming ceremonially objectionable, the expenses had ultimately to be assumed by the Department of State.

The work among the corpses brought innumerable gruesome and moving sights and incidents. The temporary morgues were at the Town Hall, the Cunard Wharf and a disused ship chandlery on Harbor Row; and the survivors exhibited a general distaste for visiting these places to identify such bodies as they might be able to. The morgues were all three very dimly lighted, and were invariably filled with silent police officers making up lists of descriptions and effects, and with silent or sobbing relatives of missing dead persons. I hardly think a dozen Americans could be got to give their services toward aiding in identifications; and in several cases we had to accompany these people bodily to see that they did not shirk this duty.

I saw five or six drowned women with drowned babies in their arms; and the corpse of one mother who had a dead infant clasped to each of the cold breasts which had so recently been their warm nestling-places. There was a curious effacement of social or mental distinction by death, and we often believed a corpse to be important when it turned out to be decidedly the opposite. The commonest expression was one of reassured tranquility; yet with an undertone of puzzlement or aggrievement as though some trusted friend had played a practical joke which the victim did not yet understand. And to judge from their countenances the humblest stokers and stewardesses had found the same peace and quietness, the same hereafter, as had Mr. Frohman and Dr. Pearson.

We contracted a temporary horror of any recumbent body, and especially of sleeping children, after a few days among these tiers of corpses. Several weeks after the disaster, one night out at my home, I went into a bedroom with a lighted match and came unexpectedly upon the sleeping form of my own little daughter. I give you my word I recoiled as though I had found a serpent. That innocent figure had thrust me back automatically into the presence of those poor livid little midget-corpses at which we had looked down so often among the *Lusitania* dead. Of course any one of those corpses might have been that of my young lady if we had happened to be crossing at that time. For that matter, any one of them might have been *your* daughter, reader, if your concerns had just then taken you onto the high seas, the common highway made by the Almighty for all nations.

© Copyright by British Pictorial Service

GRAVES OF THE UNIDENTIFIED VICTIMS
OF THE *LUSITANIA*, QUEENSTOWN

While careful descriptions of the unidentified dead had been taken, the matter of photographing them before interment bade fair to be overlooked for a time; but Consul Jenkins, among a multitude of inconspicuous acts of service, called attention to this need and succeeded in having a complete set of photographs made. These photographs are to be seen at the Cunard offices at Boston and New York, and have been very helpful in the identifications which have been made since the burials. All in all, the Cunard records state, only sixty-five of the *Lusitania* dead remain unidentified, although someone hundred and forty unknown bodies were originally buried in the great pits at Queenstown.

The funeral of these nameless victims took place on Monday afternoon, with a large representation of military, naval, and civil officials, and with throngs of sympathetic Irish people. The burial took place in three "mass-graves" (or collective graves) which had been dug at the western end of the Queenstown General Cemetery by volunteer squads of British soldiers under the direction of Colonel Ducrot. The Cemetery, in which lie the remains of the poet Wolfe, author of "The Burial of Sir John More," is located about three-fourths of a mile from Queenstown on the inland slope of the ridge on which Queenstown is built. A variety of religious ceremonies was in evidence at the burial, and the graves now constitute ground from which under certain superstitions the bodies can never be removed. Colonel Ducrot noted down, by means of the arbitrary numbers which had been assigned to them, the positions of all the coffins as they were lowered into place; and thus the relatives of subsequently identified dead are able to locate their bodies.

By Monday evening the most exigent of our duties to the survivors and the American identified corpses had been partially disposed of, and we turned more to the task of insuring the recovery and identification of the largest possible number of bodies still missing. The descriptions of lost persons with which the Consulate had been deluged were accordingly sorted out and arranged in three lists, relating respectively to dead American male passengers, dead American female passengers, and dead persons of other nationalities with regard to whom appeals had been made to us. These lists were first sent in typewritten carbon copies to the leading police and Coast Guard centers along the coast; and later were printed and scattered broadcast all along the shore villages from Youghal as far west and north as Sligo. Offers of rewards were included; and the hope was that bodies might be heard from which otherwise would have been regarded as not worth reporting.

In addition to these lists there were quite a few private handbills with descriptions and rewards as to specific missing individuals printed and circulated either with or without the cooperation of the Consulate. Fully a dozen such circulars must have related to deceased Americans. Mr. Walter Webb Ware, representing the Vanderbilt estate, spent a fortnight at Queenstown and along the southwestern coast; and his painstaking management of the search for Mr. Vanderbilt's body was of general value to all the relatives interested in having the coast inhabitants aroused to the desirability of searching for and reporting corpses. Mr. Ware offered, through the Consulate, a reward of four hundred pounds for the recovery of Mr. Vanderbilt's remains, a sum equally as potent to the minds of the Kerry fishers as would have been four hundred thousand pounds.

Beginning on Monday afternoon, the Cunard Company spared nothing in its efforts to salve the dead bodies still floating on the scene of the sinking or washed ashore along the coasts. Captain Dodd, marine superintendent of the Company, devoted his experienced executive ability to organizing the searching operations, and later gave the task over to a very capable supervisor in the person of Captain Manley. At times as many as six or eight specially-chartered tugs were engaged in the search, and every nook and cranny of the Irish shoreline for two hundred and fifty miles was gone over repeatedly. These operations were not discontinued until June 5th, more than four weeks after the catastrophe.

Altogether it may fairly be said that the efforts for the recovery of bodies were as thorough and intelligent as could have been humanly devised, and American relatives who have never received any news of their lost ones may rest assured that the bodies sank forever in deep water in the ocean or at least can never have reached the eye of man.

About twenty American bodies were washed ashore at various times and places, and about one-half of these were reported to the

Consulate by telegraph as a result of our circulars. Among these were the remains of Mr. Keser and his wife—found on strands at a distance of one hundred and twenty miles from one another; Mr. Shields, of Cincinnati, washed ashore at Castlegregory; Herbert Stone, found near Ballybunion; and Captain Miller, of Erie, Pennsylvania, recovered in County Galway considerably more than two hundred miles from the scene of the foundering. The wide distribution of the dead bodies, both British and American, was due partly to the winds and partly to the Gulf Stream. The latter splits itself into two branches against the southwestern corner of Ireland, one current traveling toward England along the southern coast and one going northward along the western coast. The Saturday and Sunday following the disaster were decidedly stormy, and the strong easterly winds coming from the direction of England scattered the body area and carried it westward as far as the corner of Ireland. There the northerly current took charge of the corpses and bore them up along the entire western coast.

In all cases where the bodies showed the slightest indication of Americanism the local police telegraphed to the Consulate at once; but in several cases they also found it necessary to give the remains instant burial before awaiting instructions. Alter we had cabled to America we would then be forced to procure permission for the exhumation of these bodies to be shipped to America; and both the local councils and Dublin Castle had to be consulted for this permission. The Irish authorities were very accommodating in facilitating all such operations, and in making arrangements, through the Cunard Company, for turning over the effects found on American bodies to the Consulate.

In fact no account of the *Lusitania* tragedy would be complete which neglected to pay an earnest tribute to the spirit in which the Irish people received it. The high efficiency and intelligence shown by the Royal Irish Constabulary was indeed to have been expected, from the well-known reputation of that body; but in addition we found that the leaders of the Irish people showed nothing but sympathy for the victims and revulsion at the crime. For several years these people had been in bitter controversy with the Cunard Company over the latter's attitude toward the Queenstown calls of the *Lusitania* and *Mauretania*; yet on an instant's notice they sunk their feelings in a sound-hearted impulse toward helpfulness. Ireland's love of America and detestation of Germany's atrocities received wonderful vindication. The verdict of the Kinsale coroner's jury that the *Lusitania* dead were "willfully murdered by the German Kaiser" was matched by more than a score of memorials and resolutions sent me by all the important local governmental bodies in the south of Ireland to be transmitted to President Wilson.

The bodies washed ashore on the western coast of Ireland, curiously enough, appeared late in June and early in July, long after the searching operations had been discontinued. Apparently the corpses remained below the surface of the sea for several weeks, and only floated again in sporadic instances after decomposition had made considerable progress. More than nine hundred corpses, of course, were never recovered at all. The bodies first recovered made a very strong appeal through their lifelikeness-a sort of unearthly aura of personality lent them by the *rigor mortis*. But this appeal was one to stimulate meditation and sentiment. The bodies recovered later on perhaps had a still more powerful effect upon the observer, because of their revolting condition; but in this case the reaction was emotional, almost physical.

The rigidity relaxed into an inebriate flabbiness, and the features broke down into a preposterously animal like repulsiveness. I was present as official witness to an autopsy performed on one body seventy-two days dead, but other corpses equaled it in the ravages they displayed. The faces registered every shading of the grotesque and hideous. The lips and noses were eaten away by sea birds, and the eyes gouged out into staring pools of blood. It was almost a relief when the faces became indistinguishable as such. Toward the last the flesh was wholly gone from the grinning skulls, the trunks were bloated and distended with gases, and the limbs were partially eaten away or bitten clean off by sea-creatures so that stumps of raw bone were left projecting.

This was the final phase of the disaster as we saw it at Queenstown; and I have given it to you without mincing words because it seems a peculiarly appropriate termination for the *Lusitania* "incident." The picture of a proud ship on a sunny day in lovely waters, beautiful even in her death throes, is not what the word *Lusitania* calls up in my mind. I see, and every American ought to see, scores and hundreds of corpses of men and women and little folks—some rotting in pools of blood in unnamed deal coffins, some staring wearily up past me from the damp floor of the old Town Hall, and some lying with vile disfigurements in shreds of clothing soaking with the salt ocean. But always corpses. That is what the *Lusitania* means to me—corpses. God spare humanity another Prussia!

CHAPTER VI

WHY AMERICA FIGHTS

THE WORK OF THE QUEENSTOWN CONSULATE IN CONNECTION WITH the loss of the *Lusitania* became, after the recovery of the last corpses early in July, merely a tedium of details—death certificates, custody and delivery of effects, sealing of coffins with the Consulate's seal, adjustment of freight charges and undertakers' charges, disinterment negotiations, and perpetually renewed assurance to bereaved Americans that there were no traces of their lost ones.

Two principal exculpatory arguments have been put forward by the Germans for their act in destroying without warning the innocent civilians who perished with the *Lusitania*. In the first place, they have had the effrontery to assert that the vessel was a ship of the British Navy. That this is a rank distortion and falsehood ought now to be too well known to bear repeating. The *Lusitania* was merely a reserve ship available for requisition, just as practically every fast ship in the world is today formally or informally a reserve ship of the nation to which it belongs. To use a simple illustration, she was in a position identical with that of a militia reservist working on a railway in one of our eastern states who has not been called to the colors. So long as he remains in civil life he has the full immunities of a civilian, even although the railway which he serves should habitually transport a certain proportion of munitions among other commodities. Just so the *Lusitania*, as a vessel of the British naval reserve, could by no stretch of the imagination be deemed a ship of war so long as she was pursuing her ordinary activities modified only as the war had modified every commercial activity.

This leads to the second German argument, that the part-cargo of munitions on the *Lusitania* made her a legitimate object of attack. The soundness of this plea depends upon what kind of attack is meant. No principle of international law, or any other law, has ever made any ship a legitimate object of the kind of attack perpetrated upon the *Lusitania*. If she had been signaled by a surface cruiser, it is true, and her occupants had been summoned to abandon ship for a place of safety provided by the enemy, she might have been fair prize. Even if the submarine had emerged and given warning, so that the *Lusitania's* commanders could have had the option of surrendering for the sake of the passengers, Germany might have had some technical, if smirchy, shreds of excuse. And if, upon such fair warning, the victim had chosen, and been able, to escape the Germans would have been in a dis-cernibly stronger moral position to sink her without warning on some subsequent voyage. Conceding, for argument's sake, that the Germans believed their cause both fair and exigent, and that they lacked the means to attack the ship in full conformity with inter-national usage, they might at least have done the utmost possible to regularize their conduct and render it correct; and had they done so the argument about the presence of absolute contraband on board the vessel would have retained some force.

But the Germans have frequently served up this contraband ar-gument in a different guise. The Allies are to all intents and purposes claiming, so Berlin expostulates, the right to introduce munitions into the British Isles *ad libitum,* free from submarine interference, by the mean expedient of covering them under passenger cabins, the passengers being used in just the way that "living screens" of civilians have been used by barbarians to cloak armed warriors in battle. Now if the *Lusitania* case stood alone this argument would have some rationality; albeit its logical significance would be a strange one. It would mean that every ship which carries contraband becomes *ipso facto* a combatant instead of a non-combatant, and may be attacked precisely as if it were an armed warship. Such a new departure in international law might conceivably be sponsored or supported on the ground that it would demark still more sharply than heretofore hostile operations from peaceful pursuits; and the world might sometime come to agree that munitions of war should only be carried by ships of war—extreme, nay absurd, as such an arrangement under present conditions would be.

Finally, if Germany had to feel herself constrained at all to adopt the horrible contention that a passenger ship becomes a lawful object of ruthless destruction if it admits contraband in its cargo, she need not at all events have selected the very poorest medium of making her verbal announcement of the new policy and the very wickedest means of proving her earnestness about it. For instead of an honorable—if the word were usable—diplomatic discussion by the usual channels, culminating in an open and formal avowal of the weird new *Supersittlichkeit,* Germany shrank from giving any intimation of her determination except a shabby and undignified paid advertisement in the columns of a foreign press, a proceeding so preposterous that many of her well-wishers were in doubt whether it were not a hoax cooked up to throw her into ridicule. And for her practical proof of the implacability of her intention to pursue the incredibly radical policy, instead of actually warning a few passenger ships, or instead even of torpedoing one or two comparatively small ships, Germany cold-bloodedly selected just that vessel which would involve the greatest number of passengers, and struck it down without a semblance of real warning. She could easily have managed to have her abominable resolution believed in by one or two overt acts involving less than a tithe or hundredth of the loss of life caused by the *Lusitania* crime.

Thus one by one the audacious pretenses by which Berlin has sought to cover the ugly nakedness of the crime fall away at contact with the most ordinary good-sense or decent thinking; and it becomes indubitable that actual and virulent malice and murder were in the hearts of the Prussians. As a minor factor I believe it to be true that a sordid jealousy of the great ship had been corroding the minds of German shipping magnates since the day she was built, and that their desire to "get" her had been woven by them into the Kaiser's war plans for many years. But far more important was the general German will to power at any cost; the insane ambition to smite down and exult over their adversaries; the disease-perverted dreams of proving a transcendent disdain of the slave-morality of their western neighbors; the lust to seal and certify their abysmal contempt and hatred of anything and everything except the Germans' destiny.

It is just this element of incomparable spiritual turpitude which gives to the torpedoing of the *Lusitania* its awful preeminence among the world's tragedies. Property of price and lives beyond price have been destroyed in other events, not only by acts of God but by the wretched iniquity of man; but never before has that iniquity been so inordinate. Such occurrences as the Halifax explosion and the Guatemalan earthquakes are of course wholly devoid of the moral element; but even in the Armenian massacres and similar modern and ancient crimes of depressing moral culpability there has never been approximated the intensity of spiritual sin which we cannot but recognize in the *Lusitania* horror. For the latter's perpetrators have not one of the mitigating excuses — the savage blood, the ignorance, the religious superstition — which have extenuated the crimes of Turk and Templar. The Prussians present the evil prodigy of men of enlightenment, progress and fine idealism prepensedly violating their consciences and hardening their hearts into a fierce and cold repudiation of all the principles they had themselves helped to erect toward the dignifying and vindicating of the existence of mankind.

During centuries men have been struggling, and every man knows how weakly and haltingly, to yield ever a little more and a little more heed and adherence to certain fugitive visions and intuitions which keep mercifully revisiting mortal hearts. We have striven to work the ape and tiger out, somewhat; to stumble a little higher and not slip back. We have ventured to formulate what we allude to as principles, and have tried as best we might to enshrine them, and to be loyal to whatever powers there be which they represent. And it was at the precarious net result of achievement in this direction, the rarest and fragilest heritage produced and passed on in human evolution, that the Germans struck th deadly guilt in striking at the *Lusitania*.

ND - #0159 - 270225 - C0 - 198/129/11 - PB - 9781910500248 - Matt Lamination